BLOODAXE W

ALDEN NOWLAN

BETWEEN TEARS AND LAUGHTER

BLOODAXE WORLD POETS

An international series of vital voices in world poetry, all speaking to the general reader as well as to the poetry lover – major modern writers from *Staying Alive* and its companion anthologies.

1: ALDEN NOWLAN: *Between Tears and Laughter: Selected Poems*
2: MARY OLIVER: *Wild Geese: Selected Poems*

Further titles in the series to be announced.

STAYING ALIVE SERIES

Neil Astley's international anthologies introduce new readers to contemporary poetry, with thematic selections of thoughtful and passionate poems about living in the modern world. They give existing poetry readers a much wider range of contemporary poems than other modern anthologies, including work by many poets even the keenest readers will be surprised to discover.

2002: Staying Alive: *real poems for unreal times*
2004: Being Alive: *the sequel to* Staying Alive
2006: Being Human [see *Being Alive* for details]

ALDEN NOWLAN

Between Tears and Laughter

SELECTED POEMS

BLOODAXE BOOKS

ISBN: 1 85224 629 4

First published 2004 by
Bloodaxe Books Ltd,
Highgreen,
Tarset,
Northumberland NE48 1RP.

www.bloodaxebooks.com
For further information about Bloodaxe titles
please visit our website or write to
the above address for a catalogue.

Bloodaxe Books Ltd acknowledges
the financial assistance of
Arts Council England, North East.

Cover printing by J. Thomson Colour Printers Ltd, Glasgow.

Printed in Great Britain by
Bell & Bain Limited, Glasgow.

CONTENTS

ACKNOWLEDGEMENTS

This order of poems in this edition is roughly chronological, following the date of first publication in book form. The selection is mainly drawn from *Selected Poems* by Alden Nowlan, edited by Patrick Lane & Lorna Crozier (House of Anansi Press, Toronto, 1996). The asterisked poems in the list of contents are from an earlier selection, *An Exchange of Gifts: Poems New & Selected*, edited by Robert Gibbs (Irwin Publishing, Toronto, 1985). Five poems are reprinted from other books: 'He continues to try to avoid being caught' from *I'm a stranger here myself* (Clarke, Irwin & Company, Toronto/Vancouver, 1974); 'At the Head Table', 'We found him kneeling', 'Subway Psalm' and 'A poem for Aida Flemming' from *I might not tell everybody this* (Clarke, Irwin & Company, Toronto/Vancouver, 1982). The title of this first UK edition of Alden Nowlan's work is borrowed from his 1971 collection *Between Tears and Laughter* but – apart from including some poems from that book – does not correspond to it in any other way.

The foreword and introduction by Patrick Lane and Lorna Crozier are reprinted from Anansi's *Selected Poems*. Gregory M. Cook's postscript 'The Wine of Astonishment' is an abridgement of an article first published in the *New Brunswick Reader (Telegraph-Journal)*, 27 June 1998.

For a fuller account of Alden Nowlan's life and work, two books are essential reading: *One Heart, One Way: Alden Nowlan: a writer's life* by Gregory M. Cook (Pottersfield Press, 2003) and *Alden Nowlan: Essays on His Works*, edited by Gregory M. Cook (Guernica Editions, 2004). UK readers can order these from Canada's Amazon.ca.

Foreword

Alden Nowlan was born in 1933 in Stanley, Nova Scotia. His young mother, who was 14 when Alden was born, gave him to his father and grandmother to raise. He went to school for only five years, leaving when he was 12 to work as a pulp cutter and millhand in the forests of the Maritimes. Nowlan was a child of the Depression, a time of poverty and struggle. It had a powerful effect upon him and upon his writing. During the early years he read voluminously, consuming the books in the library of Windsor, Nova Scotia. Like many Canadian writers of his generation, including Al Purdy and Milton Acorn, Nowlan was largely self-educated and read across the spectrum of literature and history.

At 19, Nowlan left the bush and got a job with a small-town paper in Hartland, New Brunswick. For the next 11 years he worked as a journalist while also writing poems and publishing them in literary journals across Canada and the United States. By the time he left Hartland in 1963 to work in Saint John for the *Telegraph-Journal* he had published five books and was generally recognised as a fine poet, one of the best of his generation. Three years later he had surgery for throat cancer, and the following year his book *Bread, Wine and Salt* won the Governor General's Award for poetry.

I first met Alden in 1967 or '68. We met at a party at his home on the hill by the University of New Brunswick. I fell quite in love with Claudine, his wife, and danced and drank, entranced by the spirit of his home and his other guests. Al Pittman and Ray Fraser were there and so was Louis Cormier. I was a young poet hardly anyone had ever heard of and he was kind to me. Towards midnight he made me an honorary Maritimer, everyone in the room solemnly raising their glasses to his bidding. At three in the morning he stripped me of the honour, calling me a West Coast intellectual and a fool. Everyone solemnly drank to that as well. By five in the morning we were all singing songs, maudlin and in our cups. I've never had an honour so bestowed and so quickly stripped away.

We met many times over the following years. I saw him last in the spring of 1983, two months before he died. He was very sick. I knew that he knew me, but he was at that point far along in the illness that would lead him to his death. I loved the man and loved his poetry It is fair to say that he was one of the beloved of this earth. I knew him as such and I treasure his memory, the moments we had together talking of poetry and life. Whether I was sitting in a chair in his living room sharing a glass of gin or a beer with him and Claudine, or sitting with him four thousand miles away, his poems spoke softly to me, moving me to a place as close to the heart as anyone has. I thank him for that.

Introduction

In the middle of the 8th century, Tu Fu wrote a poem that he dedicated to a friend and fellow writer. It voices the complaints we still hear from poets twelve hundred years later – lack of money, lack of recognition – yet the final lines offer some comfort:

> Our poems will be handed
> Down along with great dead poets'.
> We can console each other.
> At least we shall have descendants.

We think these ancient lines seem a worthy tribute to Alden Nowlan, for his descendants already include two generations. So often we have heard students say that in their studies of the classic Canadian anthologies it is Alden's work that stands out, his poems they remember and take into their lives as messages of love and wisdom. His poetry lives on in the words of many of us who write today; his voice will grace our lives for years to come.

Alden's poems continue to be published, read and talked about not only because he was a skilled craftsman and immaculate writer, but also because he had a great heart. Our literature has not produced another like him, none with the gift of such honesty and insight, and such a wry recognition of human frailties. The character that speaks in his best poems is sometimes awkward, contradictory or ashamed, but he is always genuine, and he expresses a compassion that is deeply felt. Although it is suspect to equate this speaker with the poet himself, a reader can't help but feel that it is Alden Nowlan talking. The voice in the poem, with all its flaws, uncertainties and desires, is his. In the poems of Robert Frost, to whom Nowlan has frequently been compared, we sense the poet speaking behind a mask, as if he has fabricated his avuncular, bucolic narrator who lectures us with the moral authority of his Puritan past. While Nowlan shares Frost's plain speech and his fascination with rural prejudices and values, he chose a different tact; he comes out of that same Northeastern Puritanism, but his voice rings with humility, self-doubt and tenderness, a tone that never betrays the heart. In later poems, such as 'Great Things Have Happened' (*see page* 133), he speaks so clearly and directly that he might be sitting at your kitchen table, glass in hand, simply talking. How privileged a reader feels to be in the presence of such intimate, eloquent stories.

This lack of distance between the man and his words was not always the case. Nowlan's early poems, shaped as they are by strict rhyme and metre, are more restrained and formal, but their subject-matter rises directly out of the world in which he grew up; small-town rural Nova Scotia and New Brunswick. Though Nowlan writes of the people and places where he lived, in these early pieces he is far from the common speech he utilises later. In 'Warren Pryor' (29), a poem reminiscent of Edwin Arlington Robinson's 'Richard Cory', Nowlan writes of a young man whose parents have laboured to free him from the hard work and poverty of the farm, 'the meagre acreage that bore them down'. Warren Pryor graduates from school to work in the bank, 'saved / from their thistle-strewn farm and its red dirt'. Nowlan skilfully uses concurrent stresses and masculine end-rhymes to create the angry tension that culminates in the last stanza:

> And he said nothing. Hard and serious
> like a young bear inside his teller's cage,
> his axe-hewn hands upon the paper bills
> aching with empty strength and throttled rage.

Nowlan's more distanced stance in the poems that make up his first four books cannot be equated with objectivity. Without a doubt, this writer cares about his subjects and does not withdraw himself from the emotional impact of their experiences; yet his choice of form and point of view keep him slightly removed. It was in the late 1950s that Nowlan's style began to change. His friend and fellow poet Robert Gibbs explains this shift in his introduction to the 1985 edition of Nowlan's selected poems, *An Exchange of Gifts*. Gibbs writes: 'In his mature verse Nowlan reaches toward pure poetry, what might be called unmediated speech. Its simplicity is that of truth, the poet's own truth, as purely stated as it can be.' With this change in voice came a more open form, the lines freed from the constraints of more formal verse. These innovations in speech and style couldn't help but affect his subject-matter. As Gibbs states, 'The freedom he acquired…to move between language at its most heightened and distanced to language at its most simple was essential to the growth of the matter of his poetry. Changes in style were changes in perception, in understanding…'

By the publication of his fifth book, *The Things Which Are*, Nowlan had become more intimate with his subjects and more forgiving of himself and others. In the poem 'The Grove Beyond the Barley' (40), he writes of coming upon a naked girl sleeping. The hapless voyeur is a character he is fond of. Here, and in many poems that follow, he is a man come upon a gentle intimacy that both startles and delights. He watches the girl for a moment, and before turning away from her he says:

>   …I hope you do not waken,
> before I go; one who chooses
> so dark a place
> to lie naked
> might cry out. The shadows quicken,
> I wish you a lover,
> dreams of sunlit meadows,
> imagine myself a gentle satyr.

In transitional poems like this, Alden seems to be delighting in his exploration of the line as a unit of meaning and rhythm freed from the restrictions of accentual-syllabic verse. He begins to play upon a dramatic order. Each line moves with the phrasing of speech, forming a kind of music that bears down upon the way we talk intimately to one another. The lines become more concentrated and distilled, forcing us to pay attention, as if someone were speaking in a voice as close to the soul as it can get. Nowlan makes us want to listen closely. Like William Carlos Williams, whom he read with care and admiration, he is not outside his subject, but inside what he observes – the most dangerous and vulnerable place to be.

Robert Bly, in his introduction to Nowlan's first selected poems, *Playing the Jesus Game*, speaks of Nowlan's courage, a quality we don't often talk about when we discuss poetry. Bly berates the false optimism of much American verse. The alternative, he writes, is 'to allow the fear or fears to come forward into the poem unconquered'. Bly claims that Nowlan does this in Canadian poetry, remarking, 'I think his work is the work of a brave man.' Bly further explains Nowlan's appeal: '…his details are fantastically clear. His clear direct language is not transformative – it's not about one thing changing into another – but a descriptive language, about the way things are.' This description is true of most of Nowlan's poetry, and if the poet had done nothing else but show us the way things are that surely would have been enough.

There are many poems, however, that we would call transformative; among them are 'Party at Bannon Brook' (34), 'The First Stirring of the Beasts' (67) and 'I, Icarus' (44). All three take us deep into the mystery of change. In the first, Nowlan speaks of moments when we try to reach past our own isolation to a sense of unity we feel but cannot utter; in the last, he writes of shape shifting and longing; and in 'The First Stirring of the Beasts' (67), he touches upon the numinous animal world that we, isolated in our own skin, cannot understand. The transformation poems are among his finest work, for they lead us beyond the edge of our knowing to a place where we touch the gods, a dark world that resides just beyond our hands. 'Party at Bannon Brook' (34) brings forth the fear Bly speaks of and leaves us with a haunting sense of primeval power and human dread:

> but because I am afraid. If we could do what we wish,
> always, I would tell them I understand:
> this is the season
> when the bobcat is not driven away
> by smoke, and the eagle
> makes reconnaissance from the coast.

The vast majority of Nowlan's poems explore the everyday, the lives of people whom he often identifies by name. There is Janice Smith in 'All Down the Morning' (22), whose husband beats her because her beauty and sensuality enrage the Puritan sensibilities of their town; there is Mary Talbot, who brings flowers to her own grave, ready and waiting beside her husband in the Hainesville Cemetery (23). There are Aunt Jane (23), Georgie and Fenwick Cranston (30), the elusive Nancy (33) and eight generations of Hungerfords, McGards and Staceys (39). Nowlan's ability to individualise, to put flesh and bone in the lines of his poetry, is raised to the level of genius in 'Ypres: 1915' (62). In an amazing *tour de force*, he ranges through the history of that place: the Moors fleeing, the French 'weeping / at the dishonour of it all', the Canadians marching straight for the lines and their imminent deaths in the carnage of shells and gas. The terror of that time and the courage of the Canadians are brilliantly and quietly brought home when the poet moves away from the larger ideas he has developed and centres everything upon one soldier:

> Private MacNally thinking:
> You squareheaded sons of bitches,
> you want this God damn trench
> you're going to have to take it away
> from Billy MacNally
> of the South End of Saint John, New Brunswick.

When Nowlan read the poem out loud, these lines were rich with the accent of the Maritimes, that long drawing out of the vowels, that sureness of speech, that simplicity of statement. Nowlan's poems about people look deeply and lovingly at those who deserve such a look, but his gaze can also be critical, almost judgemental. Woe to those who speak from a lofty place, whether from the privilege of class or a higher education, as in 'The Social Worker's Poem' (105) and 'A Mug's Game' (48). He is most critical of those who would deny the beauties of the flesh, the contradictions of being human and the sanctity of the innocent – outcasts like the Jelly Bean Man (108), who gives children candy 'from no other motive than love'. Unlike the morally superior people he debunks, he admits his own awkward stumbling towards grace, writing openly of his innermost fears. Poems like 'Bobby Sands' (137) show us that he is a man who knows how thin the line is between good and evil.

Many of Nowlan's most moving early poems reveal the sense of shame that dogged his young life, shame arising from his out-of-wedlock conception and his mother's abandonment. In the poem 'Beginning' (25) he writes of his conception: 'From that they found most lovely, most abhorred, / my parents made me'. The poem ends with 'never in making was there brighter bliss, / followed by darker shame. Thus I was made.' That sense of shame, which revolves around women in much of his work, has more than a personal source. It is one of the characteristics of a generation that grew up in the strict moral order of the puritan Maritimes. Robert Bly talks about fear in Nowlan's poetry: the fear of weakness, of women and the 'fear of being exiled, ostracised, [and] put out'. It's easy to find all of this in the early books, but in Nowlan's later work much of the anger, bitterness and self-doubt have fallen away, and we are left with what Robert Gibbs has described as 'affirmation'. This affirmation reveals a quiet and unassuming love of his own country. After the challenge issued by Billy MacNally, 'Ypres: 1915' (62) ends with these modest, yet patriotic lines:

> And that's ridiculous, too, and nothing
> on which to found a country.
>   Still
> it makes me feel good, knowing
> that in some obscure, conclusive way
> they were connected with me
> and me with them.

It takes a fine poet to realise that such huge concepts as patriotism and love of country can be eloquently expressed by focusing everything upon a single thing, an image, an ordinary man. Earlier in this poem Nowlan says, 'Sometimes I'm not even sure that I have a country.' In many brilliant poems such as this, Nowlan writes his country into existence, exploring what it is to be Canadian. One of his shorter pieces, 'Canadian January Night' (81), catches that sense of ourselves, our long winters that seem to define who we are.

> Ice storm: the hill
> a pyramid of black crystal
> down which the cars
> slide like phosphorescent beetles
> while I, walking backwards in obedience
> to the wind, am possessed
> of the fearful knowledge
> my compatriots share
> but almost never utter:
> this is a country
> where a man can die
>   simply from being
> caught outside.

Nowlan captures in just a few lines our huge, cold country and the winters we and only a few other countries endure. The poem says something, too, of our distance from one another, the bridge we dare not cross, the reticence, the formality of our loneliness. As much as anything else, Nowlan understood loneliness and loss.

Despite these poems that so explicitly describe Canada and Canadians, for many years Nowlan was known as a 'regionalist writer', someone who, because he wrote so intimately about the people and place where he lived, was not considered a writer of the first rank. This perception has done a great disservice both to Nowlan and to Canadian poetry. Almost without exception, great writers draw their material from their own lived experiences. At their most intimate, poets come to their words with an intensity that arises from their bones, the regions of the heart. Nowlan's world is indeed made up of the local, but his neighbourhoods and streets are all settings for exploring a larger humanity. This is what makes Nowlan great. He has the power to reveal our frailties and our loves, the smallness of our behaviour and the largeness of our spirit.

In one of Nowlan's last poems, 'He Sits Down on the Floor of a School for the Retarded' (138), he tells the story of going to a school for the mentally handicapped and relates his feelings of awkwardness and helplessness at not knowing quite how to behave. A female resident sits down beside him, puts her arms around him and asks Nowlan to hold her. He is distressed and awkward, unsure of what he should do, and then he does the only human thing he can, he holds her in his arms. He says:

> It's what we all want, in the end,
> to be held, merely to be held,
> to be kissed (not necessarily with the lips,
> for every touching is a kind of kiss).
>
> Yes, it's what we all want, in the end,
> not to be worshipped, not to be admired,
> not to be famous, not to be feared,
> not even to be loved, but simply to be held.

It is the rare poet who can reach this far into his understanding of compassion and human need and speak of it so clearly. We are simple creatures, Nowlan tells us, and out of that simplicity we make our lives. At the end of the poem he says of himself, the mentally handicapped woman and anyone who reads his poems: 'We are lovers. We are two human beings / huddled together for a little while by the fire / in the Ice Age, two hundred thousand years ago.'

17

Hens

Beside the horse troughs, General Grant
swaggered and foraged in the dry manure,
that winter we had twenty-seven hens
graced with white feathers and names of heroes.

Cock of the walk, he took the choicest fodder,
and he was totem, stud and constable
until his comb and spurs were frozen, bled,
and then the hens, quite calmly, picked him dead.

The Egotist

A gushing carousel, the cock
Revolved around the axeman's block.

Sweet Christ, he kicked his severed head
And drenched the summer where he bled.

And terrible with pain, the scream
Of blood engulfed his desperate dream –

He knew (and knowing could not die)
That dawn depended on his cry.

Weakness

Old mare whose eyes
are like cracked marbles,
drools blood in her mash,
shivers in her jute blanket.

My father hates weakness worse than hail;
in the morning
    without haste
he will shoot her in the ear, once,
shovel her under in the north pasture.

Tonight
    leaving the stables,
he stands his lantern on an overturned water pail,
turns,
    cursing her for a bad bargain,
and spreads his coat
carefully over her sick shoulders.

All Down the Morning

All down the morning, women sprinkled crumbs
Of musty laughter, watching Janice Smith
In brazen languor smear her husband's lips
With public kisses, while he glared or blushed.

And when the Sunday village itched in church,
They thought of Janice, hot as Babylon,
Who lured her Jimmie to the porch and bared
His people's blanket-buried secrecies.

Or dancing to the snarl of feline strings,
Each Friday at the school, they leered at jokes
That made obscenities of her taut breasts
Against her startled husband's sweating suit.

For she was city-bred and unaware
That love was bordered by the rumpled quilts
And children bred from duty as the soil
Was ploughed to hide the seed and not for joy.

So taunted by harsh laughter, half-ashamed,
Enraged with rum and manhood late one night,
And shouting like betrayal, Jim came home
To bruise his knuckles on her shameless face.

In the Hainesville Cemetery

Not all these stones
belong to death. Here and there
you read something
like
> John Andrew Talbot, 1885–1955
> Mary, his wife, 1887–

and on decoration day
Mary will come here
and put a jam jar of water and tulips
on her own grave.

> The Talbots are people
> who make the beds before breakfast
> and set the breakfast table
> every night before they go to bed.

Aunt Jane

Aunt Jane, of whom I dreamed the nights it thundered,
was dead at ninety, buried at a hundred.
We kept her corpse a decade, hid upstairs,
where it ate porridge, slept and said its prayers.

And every night before I went to bed
they took me in to worship with the dead.
Christ Lord, if I should die before I wake,
I pray thee Lord my body take.

For Nicholas of All the Russias

Wind in a rocky country and the harvest
meagre, the sparrows eaten, all the cattle
gone with the ragged troopers, winter coming,
mother will starve for love of you and wrapping
newest and least accustomed leave him squalling
out in the hills beside the skulls of foxes,
it cold and snow in the air. Stranger, knocking
(now in this latter time even the poor
have bread and sleep on straw), what silly rumour
tells me your eyes are yellow and your lips
once rose trout-quick to suck a she-wolf's teats?

Our Lord, his peaked heir and hawk-faced daughters
are gone, although they say one severed finger
was found after the soldiers cleaned the cellar.

Beginning

From that they found most lovely, most abhorred,
my parents made me: I was born like sound
stroked from the fiddle to become the ward
of tunes played on the bear-trap and the hound.

Not one, but seven entrances they gave
each to the other, and he laid her down
the way the sun comes out. Oh, they were brave,
and then like looters in a burning town.

Their mouths left bruises, starting with the kiss
and ending with the proverb, where they stayed;
never in making was there brighter bliss,
followed by darker shame. Thus I was made.

The Belled Deer

There used to be wild deer across the river,
one of them wore a bell and no one knew
its origin and so the legends grew;
grandfather thought no natural brute was ever
as swift as that one was or half so clever.
Though every fall the hunters sought her, told
of bell-sounds like the touch of ice on gold,
they said that mortal hand would kill her never.

Nobody hunts there now; a tracker's snow,
a windless afternoon were once enough
to sweep the orchards with a rifle screen.
They wanted meat, of course, for times were tough,
but there was not a man who had not seen
the belled deer in his sights and let her go.

The Coat

My grandmother's boy is dead,
his skull fractured he did not speak
as she knelt down on the dirt road
and wept on his face, her hand under his head.

My grandmother's boy was wild
as the blackbirds in Minard's clearing.
He stood up on the pedals, yodelling;
the wind too seems to ride toward death.

My father took the corduroy coat
of my grandmother's boy and hid
it behind a beam where she found it and came
weeping with it hugged to her breast,
walking slowly under the clothes line
down the pathway beside the woodshed.

There were bloody stains and the stains of mud
almost indistinguishable on the coat,
and her black dress with its red flowers
came like a ghost berating
my father as though he'd killed.
When he took the coat from her
he was so gentle I was amazed. Afterwards
he cursed and poked the coat viciously,
using a stick to crowd it
into the kitchen fire.

Baptism

In summer-coloured dresses, six young girls
are walking in the river; they look back,
frightened and proud; a choir and a cloud
of starlings sing; in rubber boots and black
frock-coat the preacher bends them separately
under; since the up-rushing stream expands
their skirts as they go down he closes them
each time with gently disapproving hands.

Sacrament

God, I have sought you as a fox seeks chickens,
curbing my hunger with cunning.
The times I have tasted your flesh
there was no bread and wine between us,
only night and the wind beating the grass.

Warren Pryor

When every pencil meant a sacrifice
his parents boarded him at school in town,
slaving to free him from stony fields,
the meagre acreage that bore them down.

They blushed with pride when, at his graduation,
they watched him picking up the slender scroll,
his passport from the years of brutal toil
and lonely patience in a barren hole.

When he went in the Bank their cups ran over.
They marvelled how he wore a milk-white shirt
work days and jeans on Sundays. He was saved
from their thistle-strewn farm and its red dirt.

And he said nothing. Hard and serious
like a young bear inside his teller's cage,
his axe-hewn hands upon the paper bills
aching with empty strength and throttled rage.

Georgie and Fenwick

Georgie and Fenwick Cranston,
in their thirties and unmarried,
Hainesville calls them old bachelors,
live with their parents on a potato farm,
six miles north of town –
they're afraid of girls.

> Saturday nights,
> in front of the Farmers Store
> some of the girls,
> their little posteriors
> gift-wrapped in Christmas-coloured
> short pants, always stop
> to tease them.

Cecelia Cameron, pressing
so close to Fenwick his overalls
scratch her bare legs, whispers,
Fenwick, do you still love me?

> When she backs away
> her breasts ripple
> under her striped blouse,
> she puts her fists in her pockets,
> tightening her pants,
> tugging them up her thighs,
> she says, Georgie
> do you want to take me home tonight?

And everybody laughs,
except Georgie and Fenwick,
who say nothing,

their mouths open,
their eyes half-shut,
blushing, rocking back and forth
in their gum rubbers. They look
like rabbits frozen
with fear of the gun.

Christ

Aloft in a balsam fir I watched Christ go,
two crows in that same tree made human laughter.

He clambered over the log fence and crossed
the orange-yellow field, his purple skirts

swishing the grain and I could hear that sound,
so close he was, and separate the hairs

in his red beard. He passed beneath me, never
once looking up, and having reached the gate

to the hill pasture shrank smaller and smaller
becoming first a fist and then a finger

and then a fleck of purple on the hillside.
At last, at the edge of the wood, he vanished
              altogether.

Looking for Nancy

Looking for Nancy
   everywhere, I've stopped
girls in trenchcoats
and blue dresses,
   said
Nancy I've looked
   all over
   hell for you,
Nancy I've been afraid
that I'd die
before I found you.

   But there's always
   been some mistake:

a broken streetlight,
too much rum or merely
my wanting too much
for it to be her.

Party at Bannon Brook

At the dead end of a road twisting snakelike
as that out of Eden, in a hunting camp, the hoarse creek crawling
through the closed door like the wet ghost of some drowned Adam,
coughing water on the floor, I sprawl on a straw-filled bunk
and drink rum with strangers:

> The chef in his tall white hat
> and apron embroidered
> with ribald slogans,
> spears steaks with slivers
> of white pine, roaring.

Beside me, in the leaping shadows
next the rough boards of the wall, her head
resting on a calendar from which all the months
have been ripped away, leaving only
the likeness of a woman
with orange skin and a body that might have been
stretched on a rack in the dungeon
of Gilles de Rais, it has such perverse,
blasphemous proportions, a girl sits, swaying
in time with the chef's song, her sweater
pulled out at the back, my circular arm
stroking the soft fat
of her belly – not because I love her
but because I am afraid. If we could do what we wish,
always, I would tell them I understand:
this is the season
when the bobcat is not driven away
by smoke, and the eagle
makes reconnaissance from the coast.

But they will not listen.
And they could do worse: tomorrow
the chef will be cashiered, kill eight hours
sending bills to debtors and this girl
sit at a desk, addressing letters
to the brains of dead men, each a packaged pudding
shelved in cold storage, and I

in whom despair
has bred superior cunning
will escape only by long study
of how the silver beads turn to gold, falling
by my employer's window, the icicles
stroked by an amorous sun.

The Bull Moose

Down from the purple mist of trees on the mountain,
lurching through forests of white spruce and cedar,
stumbling through tamarack swamps,
came the bull moose
to be stopped at last by a pole-fenced pasture.

Too tired to turn or, perhaps, aware
there was no place left to go, he stood with the cattle.
They, scenting the musk of death, seeing his great head
like the ritual mask of a blood god, moved to the other end
of the field, and waited.

The neighbours heard of it, and by afternoon
cars lined the road. The children teased him
with alder switches and he gazed at them
like an old, tolerant collie. The women asked
if he could have escaped from a Fair.

The oldest man in the parish remembered seeing
a gelded moose yoked with an ox for plowing.
The young men snickered and tried to pour beer
down his throat, while their girl friends took their pictures.

And the bull moose let them stroke his tick-ravaged flanks,
let them pry open his jaws with bottles, let a giggling girl
plant a little purple cap
of thistles on his head.

When the wardens came, everyone agreed it was a shame
to shoot anything so shaggy and cuddlesome.
He looked like the kind of pet
women put to bed with their sons.

So they held their fire. But just as the sun dropped in the river
the bull moose gathered his strength
like a scaffolded king, straightened and lifted his horns
so that even the wardens backed away as they raised their rifles.
When he roared, people ran to their cars. All the young men
leaned on their automobile horns as he toppled.

Disguise

This is the amazing thing
that it is so easy
to fool them –
the sane bastards.

I can talk
about weather, eat,
preside at meetings
of the PTA.
They don't know.

Me foreign as a Martian.
With the third eye in my forehead!
But I comb my hair
cleverly so it doesn't show

except a little
sometimes when the wind blows.

Stoney Ridge Dance Hall

They don't like strangers.
So be careful how you smile.

Eight generations
of Hungerfords, McGards and Staceys
have lived on this ridge
like incestuous kings.
Their blood is so pure
it will not clot.

This is the only
country they know.
There are men here
who have never heard of Canada.

When they tire of dancing
they go down the road
and drink white lightning
out of the bung
of a molasses puncheon.

But they never forget
to strap on the knuckles
they've made from beer bottle
caps and leather

and there are sharp spikes
in their orange logging boots.

The Grove Beyond the Barley

This grove is too secret: one thinks of murder.
Coming upon your white body (for as yet
I do not know you, therefore have no right
to speak of discovering
you, can address myself
to your body only) seeing the disorder
of your naked limbs, the arms outstretched
like one crucified, the legs bent like a runner's,
it took me less than a second to write a novel:
the husband in the black suit
worn at his wedding, the hired man
in his shirt the colour
of a rooster's comb and, in the end, you
thrown here like an axed colt.
Then I saw your breasts: they are not asleep,
move like the shadows of leaves
stirred by the wind. I hope you do not waken,
before I go; one who chooses
so dark a place
to lie naked
might cry out. The shadows quicken,
I wish you a lover,
dreams of sunlit meadows,
imagine myself a gentle satyr.

The Execution

On the night of the execution
a man at the door
mistook me for the coroner.
'Press,' I said.

But he didn't understand. He led me
into the wrong room
where the sheriff greeted me:
'You're late, Padre.'

'You're wrong,' I told him. 'I'm Press.'
'Yes, of course, Reverend Press.'
We went down a stairway.

'Ah, Mr Ellis,' said the Deputy.
'Press!' I shouted. But he shoved me
through a black curtain.
The lights were so bright
I couldn't see the faces
of the men sitting
opposite. But, thank God, I thought
they can see me!

'Look!' I cried. 'Look at my face!
Doesn't anybody know me?'

Then a hood covered my head.
'Don't make it harder for us,' the hangman whispered.

Canadian Love Song

Your body's a small word with many meanings.
Love. If. Yes. But. Death.
Surely I will love you a little while,
perhaps as long as I have breath.

December is thirteen months long,
July's one afternoon; therefore,
lovers must outwit wool,
learn how to puncture fur.

To my love's bed, to keep her warm,
I'll carry wrapped and heated stones.
That which is comfort to the flesh
is sometimes torture to the bones.

The Migrant Hand

For how many thousands of years, for how many millions
of baskets and waggonloads and truckloads of onions,
or cotton, or turnips has this old man knelt
in the dirt of sun-crazy fields? If you ask him,
he'll put you off: he's suspicious of questions.
The truth is that Adam, a day out of Eden,
started him gathering grapes: old Pharaoh
sold him to Greece; he picked leeks for the Seljuks,
garlic for Tuscans, Goths and Normans,
pumpkins and maize for the Pilgrim Fathers,
has forgotten them all, forgotten all of the past, except
the last ten hours of blackflies and heat,
the last two hundred barrels of potatoes.

I, Icarus

There was a time when I could fly I swear it.
Perhaps, if I think hard for a moment, I can even tell you the year.
My room was on the ground floor at the rear of the house.
My bed faced a window.
Night after night I lay on my bed and willed myself to fly.
It was hard work, I can tell you.
Sometimes I lay perfectly still for an hour before I felt
     my body rising from the bed.
I rose slowly, slowly until I floated three or four feet
     above the floor.
Then, with a kind of swimming motion, I propelled myself
     toward the window.
Outside, I rose higher and higher, above the pasture fence,
     above the clothesline, above the dark, haunted trees
     beyond the pasture.
And, all the time, I heard the music of flutes.
It seemed the wind made this music.
And sometimes there were voices singing.

Sailors

Nobody younger than eighteen or older than twenty
ever combs his flair quite so neatly, nobody else
except maybe a boxer has that feverish, watchful
look when he's waiting
for a light to change, or an elevator.

This shouldn't surprise me: already, at twenty-nine,
I've learned one of the most disturbing
things about getting older
is that every year
there are more kids in the world.

Why shouldn't sailors
look like little boys
dressed in the folk costume
of some strange country?

Oh, but in Halifax, in the last war, I held my breath
like Jim Hawkins in his apple barrel, and watched them stride
down all the sidewalks, tall as Joe Palooka,
stronger than Tarzan, wiser than The Shadow,
and brave – brave as the Swiss in my Grade III reader,
brave as Thermopylae, brave as Dieppe,
        their very boots
pronouncing *Dunkirk* each time they struck the pavement.

A View from the Bridge

When the movie opens, a machine is lowering lumber into the
        hold of a ship.
We see a great raft of boards swinging from a cable high overhead;
and we know at once that the cable will break,
as it has broken in every movie we've ever seen,
and the boards will fall like a bomb, as they always do, and a man
        will scream,
and, almost before the screaming has stopped, we will hear the
        sirens,
then the running footsteps,
and the camera will zoom in and we will see the face of the
        longshoreman,
and if it is a face we do not recognise, chances are he will be dead,
but if it is the face of Kirk Douglas or Burt Lancaster or John Wayne
he will open his eyes slowly because stars never die before the end
of the last reel – knowing all this,
knowing almost the exact moment
when the cable will snap (a second after
the last credit line flashes on the screen)
it is curious we are all of us so tense and silent
  until it happens –
it is almost as it we were afraid of being cheated.
Perhaps this is a foreign film, a documentary,
even Red propaganda –
what if the cable holds?
But, of course, it never does:
in another moment we will hear the steel snap,
see the boards fall –
and almost everyone in the theatre
will breathe a little sigh of relief
as he settles back
to enjoy the show.

The Sleepwalker

Zeno of Elea said an arrow doesn't move:
it is always at rest
at one of a series
of points: so it is with a sleepwalker

who always seems to know where he's going
without knowing where he is,
the body saying
'no' to its own
movements, and the eyes
focused on something so far away
nobody can see it
without going blind
to everything between;

and when he wakes up
in his own house
in the world
where he's lived
all his life,
he says:
where am I?
how did I get here?

while the vision
darts like a fish,
signet of Christ,
cymbal of wisdom,
into the swirling
depths of his eyes.

A Mug's Game

At the party that followed the poetry reading,
one girl kept telling me how thrilled she was to meet
someone who hadn't gone to university, and another said
I reminded her so much of whoever it was who played
in *Bus Stop* she kept expecting Marilyn to walk in, and the hostess
extending three bite-size salami sandwiches
and a glass of warm whiskey and ginger ale
smiled at me like Li'l Abner's Aunt Bessie
welcoming her nephew to Toronto.

The man from the CBC, who said: 'Of course, you're staying
at the YMCA' and thought he was humouring me
by acting impressed when he found out I wasn't,

explained: 'The purpose of such readings is to give writers
from unlikely places like Hartland, New Brunswick,
the chance to communicate
with others
of their own kind.'

The Word

Though I have the gift of tongues
and can move mountains,
my words are nothing
compared with yours,
though you only
look up from my arms
and whisper my name.

This is not pride
because I know
it is not
my name that you whisper
but a sign
between us,
like the word
that was spoken
at the beginning
of the world
and will be spoken again
only when the world ends.

This is not that word
but the other
that must be spoken
over and over
while the world lasts.

Tears,
laughter,
a lifetime!
All in one word!

The word you whisper
when you look up
from my arms
and seem to say
my name.

Day's End

(for Anne)

I have worked since daylight in the hayfields.
We walked home at dusk, following the horses.
For supper, I ate hot bread and spiced ham,
    onions and tomatoes.
Now I kneel over a basin of cold water
and a woman washes my hair –
a strong woman whose knuckles rake my scalp.
Her hands smell of soap, I am naked to the waist,
    she leans her weight against me;
laughs huskily when I seize her wrists
    and try to push away her hands.
I am young and strong but a great weariness is upon me –
I would be willing to die now if I were sure that death is sleep.

In the Operating Room

The anesthetist is singing
'Michael, row the boat ashore,
Hallelujah!'
And I am astonished
that his arms
are so hairy –
thick, red, curly hair
like little coppery ferns
growing out of
his flesh
from wrist
to shoulder.
I would like
to reach up
and touch
the hairy arm
of the anesthetist
because it may be
the last living thing
I will ever see
and I am glad
it is not
white and hairless
– but if I reached up
and wound
a few wisps
of his hair
around my forefinger
as I would like to do
they would think
their drugs
had made me silly
and might remember
and laugh
if I live,

so I concentrate
very hard
on the song
the anesthetist
is singing –
'The River Jordan
is muddy and cold,
Hallelujah!'
And soon
everything
is dark
and nothing
matters
and when I try
to reach up
and touch
the hair
which I think of
now as
little jets
of fire,
I discover
they've strapped
my arms
to the table.

Morning of the Third Operation

Thinking,
just as I
blacked out:
what if all
the evidence
is wrong,
what if
the dead
look on
but can't
make us
understand,
what if
I die
and go home
and Claudine
is crying:
will she know
what it means
even if I
have the strength
to knock
a pencil
off the table.
Listen, Claudine,
look at me!
I'm alive!
Don't be
so damned
stupid, woman.
I'm here
beside you.
But she keeps on
crying
and then

a friend comes
and takes her away
because it isn't good
for her
to be alone.

Escape from Eden

When I was near death,
these little nurses
stripped me naked
and bathed me.
When it appeared
I would live,
they covered
my loins
with a sheet.
When I learned to sit up
and drink consommé
through a straw,
they somehow managed
to wash my back
without removing
my pajama jacket.
Now that I can walk
to the sink and back
without falling,
they knock loudly,
pause,
before slowly opening
the door
of my room.

The Mysterious Naked Man

A mysterious naked man has been reported
on Cranston Avenue. The police are performing
the usual ceremonies with coloured lights and sirens.
Almost everyone is outdoors and strangers are conversing excitedly
as they do during disasters when their involvement is peripheral.
'What did he look like?' the lieutenant is asking.
'I don't know,' says the witness. 'He was naked.'
There is talk of dogs – this is no ordinary case
of indecent exposure, the man has been seen
a dozen times since the milkman spotted him and now
the sky is turning purple and voices
carry a long way and the children
have gone a little crazy as they often do at dusk
and cars are arriving
from other sections of the city.
And the mysterious naked man
is kneeling behind a garbage can or lying on his belly
in somebody's garden
or maybe even hiding in the branches of a tree,
where the wind from the harbour
whips at his naked body,
and by now he's probably done
whatever it was he wanted to do
and wishes he could go to sleep
or die
or take to the air like Superman.

Country Full of Christmas

Country full of Christmas,
the stripped, suspicious elms
groping for the dun sky –
what can I give my love?

The remembrance – mouse hawks
scudding on the dykes, above
the wild roses; horses and cattle
separate in the same field.
It is not for my love.

Do you know that foxes
believe in nothing
but themselves – everything
is a fox disguised: men, dogs and rabbits.

The Mosherville Road

If a man wishes to be sure of the road he treads on,
he must close his eyes and walk in the dark.

ST JOHN OF THE CROSS

It is nowhere so dark
   as in the country
      where I was born.
I remember nights
   I held my hand
      an inch from my eyes
and saw nothing.
   Yet I kept putting one
      foot in front of the other
and don't recall ever falling
   into the ditch,
      though I was so aware
of it, three feet deep,
   on both sides of me
      with gravel walls
and filthy water
   at the bottom of it,
      that it seems to me now
I must have gone into it,
   at least once
      and forgotten. There was glass
from broken bottles
   and everything else
      that gets thrown from cars
in that ditch and thorn bushes grew
   on the opposite side of it,
      and there were trees
and night birds
   and flying insects
      I couldn't see.

Usually I talked
    to myself and sometimes I sang
        as I stumbled along
and it wasn't until tonight
    almost twenty years
        later I began to realise
how much I was afraid.

Hymn to Dionysus

The trick is to loose
    the wild bear
        but hold tight
to the chain,
    woe
        when the bear
snatches up
    the links
        and the man dances.

A Poem About Miracles

Why don't records go blank
the instant the singer dies?
Oh, I know there are explanations,
but they don't convince me.
I'm still surprised
when I hear the dead singing.
As for orchestras,
I expect the instruments
to fall silent one by one
as the musicians succumb
to cancer and heart disease
so that toward the end
I turn on a disc
labelled *Götterdammerung*
and all that comes out
is the sound of one sick old man
scraping a shaky bow
across an out-of-tune fiddle.

Ypres: 1915

The age of trumpets is passed, the banners hang
like dead crows, tattered and black,
rotting into nothingness on cathedral walls.
In the crypt of St Paul's I had all the wrong thoughts,
wondered if there was anything left of Nelson
or Wellington, and even wished
I could pry open their tombs and look,
then was ashamed
of such morbid childishness, and almost afraid.

I know the picture is as much a forgery
as the Protocols of Zion, yet it outdistances
more plausible fictions: newsreels, regimental histories,
biographies of Earl Haig.
                              It is always morning
and the sky somehow manages to be red
though the picture is in black and white.
There is a long road over flat country,
shell holes, the debris of houses,
a gun carriage overturned in a field,
the bodies of men and horses,
but only a few of them and those
always neat and distant.
                              The Moors are running
down the right side of the road.
The Moors are running
in their baggy pants and Santa Claus caps.
The Moors are running.
                              And their officers,
Frenchmen who remember
Alsace and Lorraine,
are running backwards in front of them,
waving their swords, trying to drive them back,
weeping
          at the dishonour of it all.

The Moors are running.

And on the left side of the same road,
the Canadians are marching
in the opposite direction.

The Canadians are marching
in English uniforms behind
a piper playing 'Scotland the Brave'.

The Canadians are marching
in impecccable formation,
every man in step.

The Canadians are marching.

And I know this belongs
with Lord Kitchener's moustache
and old movies in which the Kaiser and his general staff
seem to run like the Keystone Cops.

That old man on television last night,
a farmer or fisherman by the sound of him,
revisiting Vimy Ridge, and they asked him
what it was like, and he said,
There was water up to our middles, yes
and there was rats, and yes
there was water up to our middles
and rats, all right enough,
and to tell you the truth
after the first three or four days
I started to get a little disgusted.

Oh, I know they were mercenaries
in a war that hardly concerned us.
I know all that.

Sometimes I'm not even sure that I have a country.

But I know they stood there at Ypres
the first time the Germans used gas,
that they were almost the only troops
in that section of the front
who did not break and run,
who held the line.

Perhaps they were too scared to run.
Perhaps they didn't know any better
– that is possible, they were so innocent,
those farmboys and mechanics, you have only to look
at old pictures and see how they smiled.
Perhaps they were too shy
to walk out on anybody, even Death.
Perhaps their only motivation
was a stubborn disinclination.

Private MacNally thinking:
You squareheaded sons of bitches,
you want this God damn trench
you're going to have to take it away
from Billy MacNally
of the South End of Saint John, New Brunswick.

And that's ridiculous, too, and nothing
on which to found a country.
                              Still
it makes me feel good, knowing
that in some obscure, conclusive way
they were connected with me
and me with them.

On the Nature of Human Compassion

I said to a herring gull with a broken wing:
Bird, I am sad for you.
If I could make you trust me
I'd take you up in my hands,
carry you back to the city
and hire a veterinarian to heal you.
Or if my stomach were stronger
I'd use a stone or a club of driftwood
to shorten your death.
                    And the herring gull answered:
Man, you are not sad for me,
but for yourself, so great an egotist
you can put on the body of a bird
or play Mephistopheles to a housefly,
what you call your compassion the conceit
that all living things are Alden Nowlan in disguise.

A Black Plastic Button and a Yellow Yoyo

I wish I could make her understand
her child isn't the Christ Child
and didn't create the world,
then maybe she'd stop shaking
her fists in his face
and he could come out from inside
his yellow yoyo
or black plastic button
because that's where he hides:
I've watched from my window,
unable to write because of her screaming,
and seen him flying out of his body
into the yoyo,
where he can neither see nor be seen,
neither hear nor speak,
a Buddha smaller than my thumb,
a sleeping Krishna,
there inside that dancing yoyo;
and if she knocks it from his hand,
why, he simply turns
the second button from the top
of his windbreaker,
a black plastic button,
turns it between
his thumb and forefinger,
focuses his eyes on it,
until he is safe again,
curled up in a ball
where nothing at all can reach him.

The First Stirring of the Beasts

The first stirring of the beasts
is heard at two or three or four
in the morning, depending on the season.

You lie, warm and drowsy, listening,
wondering how there is so much difference
between the sounds
cattle and horses make,
moving in their stanchions or halters,
so much difference that you can't explain,
so that if someone asked you
which of them is moving now?
you couldn't answer
but lying there, not quite awake,
you know, although it doesn't matter,
and then a rooster crows
and it sounds, or maybe you imagine this,
unsure and a little afraid,
                              and after a little
there are only the sounds of night
that we call silence.

The second stirring of the beasts
is the one everybody understands.
You hear it at dawn
and if you belong here
you get up.
Anyway, there is no mystery
in it, it is the other stirring,
the first brief restlessness
which seems to come for no reason
that makes you ask yourself
what are they awake for?

Chance Encounter

There is something odd in the road ahead.
A man in a black coat walking a dog,
a tall man in a long black coat walking a big red dog,
or is it a black mare with a red colt.
                                        God
don't let me hit them.
                          I don't like
to be splashed by death.
                          The car stops in time
and I roll down the window.
                          There is a cow moose
standing not ten feet away
and her calf a little farther off,
neither of them knowing what to make of the headlights,
bright as lightning, solid as the light
of a full moon on a cloudless night.
Then the cow crosses over, very slowly,
not looking back
until she reaches
the edge of the woods
on the other side
and finds the calf has not followed her,
                                        but gone back
and they look at one another
across the light that separates them
and perhaps she makes little coaxing sounds I can't hear,
while I will him
not to run away where they might never find each other
but to be brave enough
to walk into the light
I don't dare turn off
for fear of humans like myself
– and at last he begins to walk
toward the road
                and after a moment's pause

68

enters the light
                    and crosses it
in about thirty seconds,
                              a long time
when you're holding your breath,
                                      and the instant
he's safely over, she runs and he
    runs behind her,
        and I drive on,
                              happy about it all,
bursting to tell someone about the great sight I've seen,
yet not even sure why it should seem so important.

An Exchange of Gifts

As long as you read this poem
I will be writing it.
I am writing it here and now
before your eyes,
although you can't see me.
Perhaps you'll dismiss this
as a verbal trick,
the joke is you're wrong;
the real trick
is your pretending
this is something
fixed and solid,
external to us both.
I tell you better:
I will keep on
writing this poem for you
even after I'm dead.

Fair Warning

I keep a lunatic chained
to a beam in the attic. He
is my twin brother whom
I'm trying to cheat
out of his inheritance.
It's all right for me
to tell you this because
you won't believe it.
Nobody believes anything
that's put in a poem.
I could confess to
murder and as long as
I did it in a verse
there's not a court
that would convict me.
So if you're ever
a guest overnight
in my house, don't
go looking for
the source of any
unusual sounds.

Friends

On nights like this
I wish I had a friend
or better yet two
friends, a man and a woman,
who knew me better
than they knew each other,
who would talk but
not talk too much,
who would make me laugh
and laugh with me,
who would say something
to surprise me
occasionally but
only occasionally,
who would not
think of conversation
as putty with which
to plug the silences
or as chess played
with invisible pieces
on an invisible board,
and who, above all,
were content in
my clothes closet or
in the basement
behind the furnace
where they'd stay
while I worked
or slept or was happier
alone;
      on a night like this
I could go upstairs or
go down and

poke my head around
the furnace, say
to them: 'Hey! Wake up!
I'm lonesome.'

The Married Man's Poem

Five years married
and he has never once
wished he dared kill her,
                    which means
they're happy enough.
But it isn't love.

Mistaken Identity

It's good sometimes
to be mistaken for
someone else, although
it usually ends
badly.
      Getting down from
a bus in Boston
in 1951, when I was
seventeen, I stepped
into the arms of
a fat woman whose
breath smelled of
beer, and she kissed
me on the mouth and
said, Walter, Walter,
and I was so lonesome
that for a second I
was almost tempted
to pass myself
off as whoever she
thought I was; but
what I did was
mumble something
about there being
a mistake, and even
before I spoke she
had realised that
and was pushing
me away.
      Another time
a beautiful young girl
blew a kiss at me
from the open window
of a cab in New Haven,

Connecticut, and
shouted, Hi, Davie!
She wore a red scarf,
I remember. And I waved.
Then because I wanted
her to keep smiling
at me, lovingly, I
very quickly
turned away.

The Iconotrophic Instant
(for Robert Cockburn)

The old remember everything:
nothing is lost.
                   If your lover outlives you
by half a century and when asked your name
cannot recall it, names are less important
than your falling in the snow that night,
near a bonfire or under a neon light,
and rolling in it like a child
though you were already
the mother of his children.
He never tires of telling it:
'Once, I remember, she slipped
on an ice patch, fell down and rolled over and over
like a kitten or a puppy.'
Those who care for his needs
wink at one another, they do not know
he has told them the whole story
of his love for you, of your love for him.
And that old soldier
in the hundred-year-old diary
of an English curate:
                   Talking of wolves,
he said he remembered,
how every night they came down to drink from the river,
four or five of them, like mastiffs and as big.
The soldiers used to scare them
by snapping the locks
of their flint muskets, making the powder flash.
When the wolves saw it they went away.
They did not like to see that.
'It is nothing to write,' the curate wrote,
yet he was wise enough

to record it twice in five months
during which he must have heard it
scores of times.
                    It was one man's history
of the Peninsular men who followed hook-nosed Atty,
not yet Wellington, into Portugal, through Spain,
    across the Pyrenees.

He Raids the Refrigerator and Reflects on Parenthood

Nowlan, you maudlin boob,
almost blubbering because
two hours ago at the party
your son said, I'll be
fifteen tomorrow, can I
have a whole pint of beer?
Grinning so he could say
it was a joke if you
took it that way; but he
was serious all right:
it's like music sometimes
how serious he can be
about small matters
which you're thereby
reminded were
important.
                And you hesitated,
not because you ever
considered refusing
but because you wanted him
to know that you, too,
value rituals. But
there were only enough
cool ones for the guests.
So you gave him a warm one.
It doesn't matter, he said.
It's okay. But of course it did.
The rite was spoiled
by an imperfection. And now he's
asleep upstairs and you're
holding open the door
of the refrigerator, contemplating
a pint bottle with no more

than two ounces taken from it
and the cap put back so well
you'd need an opener
to take it off again, thinking
of the petty treason
we commit so often
against those we love,
the confidence games
in which parents play
their children for suckers.

Johnnie's Poem

Look! I've written a poem!
Johnnie says
and hands it to me
        and it's about
        his grandfather dying
        last summer, and me
        in the hospital
and I want to cry,
don't you see, because it doesn't matter
if it's not very good:
        what matters is he knows
and it was me, his father, who told him
        you write poems about what
        you feel deepest and hardest.

Canadian January Night

Ice storm: the hill
a pyramid of black crystal
down which the cars
slide like phosphorescent beetles
while I, walking backwards in obedience
to the wind, am possessed
of the fearful knowledge
my compatriots share
but almost never utter:
this is a country
where a man can die
                              simply from being
caught outside.

Cornflowers

I am a saint with a broken wing
        who shakes his fists like the wind.
                                    You
are the homecoming
              of the sun,
                            an hurrah of grass.
The cornflowers are not yet
        aware they will die soon
                from last night's frost.
They are like the Empress
Elizabeth of Austria
who was stabbed with a blade so thin
she continued to smile
                  and did not interrupt
her walk,
        although it had pierced her heart.
Since in this place and season
        they are the only flowers
                that do not ask for money
I give you them.
                Nothing else is beautiful
this hunchbacked October night
except the moon.

Written While Waiting for Another Chest X-Ray

I don't want to die.
That sounds like something said
by one of the more stupid
19th century kings, some Maximilian or Ferdinand
who in his youth admired Byron
and nibbled the ears
of the prettier page boys, in middle age
turned to brandy and took communion
every morning of his life,
grew enormously fat and
in his sixtieth year
summoned a cardinal, said, Your Eminence,
I don't want to die, see that the matter
is taken care of,
               and with that
went shooting grouse
and killed more than one hundred,
being a most excellent shot.

For Yukio Mishima

...The novelist, often mentioned as a possible Nobel Prize winner,
stripped to his waist, unbuttoned his trousers and sat down on
the floor of the room. He touched his stomach, gave a piercing yell
and drove his short samurai sword into himself...

NEWS ITEM

You can't hear me, Yukio Mishima. But, then,
a man who addresses the dead is bound to discover,
sooner or later, that he's talking to himself.
The newspapers argue whether
you were certifiably insane
or a buffoon for whom suicide
was the only bit of egocentricity
that remained untasted.
They can't find words for you
as they could readily had done
if you'd decapitated yourself
while driving a racing car
or in any other equally extravagant
but fashionable manner;
just as they couldn't admit
it was a bull that got Hemingway:
there were hoofprints leading away
from the lodge where his body lay
that had dripped from the horns.
That was never published.
But perhaps I understand you better than most,
Yukio Mishima, wanting to restore the sword
to its place beside the chrysanthemums.
The worst way to die
is as a prisoner, at the hands
of a pitiless human enemy.
                              Next to the worst
is death of natural causes.
There are no pacifists
in the cancer ward.

That great war chief
whose people called him *Our Strange Man*
and whom the whites called Crazy Horse,
led his soldiers into battle shouting:
'Come on, Lakota, it's a good day to die!'
My grandfather left
an imitation leather cardboard wallet
containing a Junior G-Man secret pocket,
five greenish pennies, and a will beginning:
'I, Cathal O Nuallain, Prince of Fortara...'
Myself, delirious, coming out from under
the ether and into the demerol
like a man crawling out of the sea
and into the jungle,
resolved to die like
an Irish prince: an old man's foolishness,
a small boy's games
dignifying the fear, almost
sanctifying the pain.

Old Town Revisited

I will park on the corner in front
of the furniture store. The day I left
eight years ago, Moses Timmins stood
across the street, on the top step
to the post office. He waved goodbye.
When I went back
for the first time, a year
later, I found he had descended
only one step (there are five)
and was still waving. I'm
telling you the truth. He had moved
less than a foot in twelve months.
This morning, though, he should be
about to put his foot on the sidewalk.
And Henry Ferguson may have finished
closing the door of The Dough Boy Diner
– he was about to touch
the inside handle eight years ago,
and last summer he was almost
outside, but had paused to say
a final word to Mary-Beth MacGuire,
who when I see her next will be washing
the mug she was starting to fill
in 1963 for Standish Morehouse who will
be getting up from his stool to go back
to the office – how many years
I wonder will it take him
to walk that hundred yards? I foresee
myself an old man on his last visit,
leaning on the shoulder of a grown
grandson who may not even be born
twenty years from now, the pair of us
getting out at this same corner. I foresee

Moses, Standish and Henry finally
come near enough to resume
whatever conversations my
first departure interrupted.

The Encounter, the Recognition

There's a path through the woods, or a corridor
in an empty building. I enter it
at both ends and walk slowly toward myself.
I am wholly drunk.
                        I am wholly sober.
We meet midway
                        and recognise one another.
'Hello, Alden,' I say.

That's how my best poems are created.

They Go Off to Seek Their Fortunes

*The three largest immigrant colonies in Toronto consist
of the Italians, the Portuguese and the Maritimers.*
A TORONTONIAN IN CONVERSATION

They have their pictures taken, peering at maps.
They stop along the road to buy beer, opening
the bottles in ways peculiar to them:
the tough one uses his teeth, the cool one his belt buckle,
the mouth organ player takes a bottle in each hand,
hooks the caps together and pulls
so that only one comes off.
                                    They tell strangers
where they're from and where they're going and how much
their second cousins make in Sudbury. They say,
'I'm from the island,' or 'I'm from the bay,'
as if there were only one of each in the world.
They wear white socks and copper bracelets.
They light matches on their thumbnails.
                                    They spit.
When they're happy they whoop and when they're sad
they can be dangerous. They're almost never
neutral toward anyone – they either like you
or are prepared quite simply to kick
the living Jesus out of you.
                                    They are warriors
for whom it's natural to bid goodbye
with a kind of mock military salute.
                                    They greet one another
with a meaningful movement that is part
bow, part shrug, part nod, accompanied
by a slight pursing of the lips,
the barest suggestion of a wink.

For My Grandchildren, as Yet Unborn

For my grandchildren
who will never know
the beasts of the fields:
my own grandmother
would call from the pasture
gate, 'So-Boss! So-Boss!'
It would be dusk, and the cattle
a half-mile away in the trees,
but Old Mother Whitehead,
leader of the cows, would hear her
and come with the others behind her,
not that she cared
whether they followed,
she alone among them
went where she pleased.
Creeters, my grandmother said,
which meant *creatures* which meant *cows*.
And they'd walk not at all
as they'd walked that morning;
they'd come slowly,
slowly, but not stopping;
it was even
a little frightening
the way they came
out of the woods
and down the hill,
so purposeful they seemed,
Old Mother leading them.

He Takes His Leave

It was as if I'd opened
Grimms' Fairy Tales and lowered myself into
one of the illustrations, become
the stripling taking his leave
of his village, on foot, with a rucksack
containing his other shirt, except I
carried a black cardboard suitcase
and boarded the train, after walking
only two miles: it didn't stop there
unless you raised a flag or,
to be more accurate, fetched from
the waiting room a broomstick
to which a green and grey rag had been
tacked, stood on tiptoe and
shoved it in a rusty iron socket.
The road was muddier
than I had ever seen it
that March day in 1952; I sank
to my ankles, once or twice it
sucked off my shoe.
An old woman emptying slops
called after me, said that she'd pray for me.
Her name was Lilah.
I patted the head
of a half-wild dog.
The wind smelled of sea-salt and sawdust.
I pause at this point to ask
myself if this matters to anyone,
including its author, and decide
at last that it must, if for no other reason
than this: now, nineteen years later,
I sometimes have nightmares in which
it's that same day, but the train
doesn't stop, all the roads are flooded

or blocked with snow, and even
the telephone lines are down,
or, more mysteriously,
the village has been transformed
into an island and there will never be
another boat to the mainland.
When I wake up
the pillow is damp with sweat,
my hands are shaking.

On Being Detested by a Friend

I know of only one person I like
who detests me. There could be others.

I like him better
each time I learn
that he's tried again
to injure me.

He does it so clumsily
it's obvious he's never
done it to anyone before

and afterwards he
despises himself;
his grin is ghastly
with guilt when we

come face to face
and must talk.
This happens
once or twice a month:
ours is a small city.

I don't think he knows
that I know he detests me
but I'm almost sure
he knows I like him

and is miserable
because of this.

I wonder if there's
anyone I detest
who likes me?
I think I would like him.

Land and Sea

Old men repeat themselves.
In other words: speak songs.

Can't let the sea be,
the land can't.
                    Won't ever
leave her in peace.
                    Has to keep
troubling the waters,
the land does.
                    This from
Captain Thorburn Greenough
of Hall's Harbour who, in his prime,
could have sailed a bucket
through hell with his handkerchief,
they say

The land won't let the sea be.

You'd of sailed under
canvas, you'd of knowed that.
Wouldn't of needed me
to tell you.
                    The shore!
We never felt safe
till we was out of her reach.

Full Circle

In my youth, no one spoke of love
where I lived, except I spoke of it,
and then only in the dark. The word was known
like the name of a city on another continent.
No one called anyone his friend,
although they had friends. Perhaps they were afraid
to commit so much of themselves,
to demand so much of others; for if they'd said,
'We're friends,' as they never did,
it would have been a contract.
As it was, they could quarrel,
even hit one another if they were drunk,
and remain friends, never having said it.
Where nothing was sworn there could be no betrayal.
Nor did they touch
casually; their persons seemed to occupy
more space than their bodies did.
Seeing an adult run we'd have looked first for the reason
in the direction from which he came. We never met trains;
my people were like that.
                          It was not enough for me.
'I love you,' I said.
Whispered it, painfully, and was laughed at;
hid until the wounds healed and said it again,
          muttered it.
Wanting to be loved, 'I love you,' was what I said.
And I learned to touch, as a legless man
learns to walk again.
                          Came to live among people
who called anyone a friend
who was not an enemy, to whom there were no strangers:
because there were so many, they were invisible.

Now, like everyone else, I send
postcards to acquaintances, With Love –
Love meaning, I suppose, that I remember the recipients
kindly and wish them well. But I say it
less often and will not be surprised
at myself if the time comes when I do not say it,
when I do not touch, except desperately, when I ask
nothing more of others, but greet them with a wink,
as my grandfather might have done, looking up
for an instant from his carpenter's bench.

The Red Wool Shirt

I was hanging out my wash,
says the woman in North Sydney.
It was a rope line I was using
and they were wooden pins,
the real old-fashioned kind
that didn't have a spring.

It was good drying weather.

I could see the weir fishermen
at work.
          I had a red wool shirt
in my hands and had just
noticed that one of the buttons
was missing.

Then I looked up and saw
Charlie Sullivan coming
towards me.
He'd always had a funny walk.
It was as if he was walking
sideways.
          That walk of his
always made me smile except
for some reason
I didn't smile
that day.
          He had on a hat
with salmon flies
that he'd tied himself
in the brim.

Poor old Charlie.

It's bad, Mary, he said.

I finished
hanging up the red wool
shirt
        and then I said,
Charlie, it's not
both of them, and he said,
Mary, I'm afraid it is.

And that was that.

What Colour Is Manitoba?

My son, in Grade III or IV
and assigned to make a map,
asked us what colour is
Manitoba? and refused to believe
it didn't matter, provided
it wasn't the same
as Saskatchewan and Ontario.
I remember his face.
I've seldom observed
such constrained rage
except in small children
and university professors.

But it's a common failing,
this excessive faith
in one method of denoting
boundaries. In his atlas
at school, Manitoba was
purple-brown. Similarly,
the road maps indicate
that I live less than
five hundred miles
from my birthplace.

There are truer charts.

I'd never once used
a telephone
in the nineteen years
before I left there,
had never eaten a hamburger;
I could milk a cow by hand
or yoke an ox, knew a man who
once as a passenger

in a heavily-loaded
stage coach inching up
one side of a very steep
hill in California
had got off to walk
and as a result of this
– the downward slope
being equally precipitous,
the horses being compelled
by the weight behind them
to gallop and he having to
run to catch up –
was mistaken by the driver
for a highwayman, and shot:
the scar was still there
after fifty years.
Little else had changed
in our village since
the mid-eighteenth century
when Coulon de Villiers
passed through with his troops,
seven years before
he defeated young George
Washington at Fort Necessity.
Scraps of grape-shot worked
their way to the surface
of the earth the way bits
of shrapnel are said to
emerge at last through the skin
of an old soldier.

Add to all this
that it wasn't the same
for everybody, even there.
My family was poor.
Not disadvantaged – curse
that word of the sniffling
middle classes, suggesting

as it does that there's
nothing worse than
not being like them.
We were poor – curse that word, too,
as a stroke victim
half-maddened by his inability
to utter a certain phrase
will say 'shit' instead
and be understood.

A sociologist,
belonging by definition to
one of the lesser
of the ruling sub-castes,
comes from Columbia University
to study a community
in Nova Scotia not very different
from where I was born.
A Tutsi witch doctor among Hutus.
He finds, according to
the *New York Times*, that
almost everyone he meets is crazy.

It's as if a chemist
had analysed a river
and declared that its water
was an inferior form of fire.

There are secrets I share
with the very old. I know why
we fought in the Boer War
and how in the lumber camps
we cracked the lice between
our thumbnails and it made
a homely sound, was a restful
occupation of an evening:
cracking lice, we were
like women knitting.

Altogether apart
from that, I bear tribal
marks, ritual mutilations.
My brothers and sisters
fill the slums of every
city in North America.
(God knows this is no boast.)
The poor, whom the Russians
used to call the Dark People,
as if it were in the blood.
I know their footsteps.
We meet each other's eyes.

If I Could Be Certain, God

If I could be certain, God, that
      you were watching us,
it would be enough. I'd ask less
      of you than an actor
asks of an audience: merely that
      you be there.

You needn't suspend the laws of
      the universe for me.
I'd be embarrassed. And the prospect
      of living for ever
would frighten me almost as much as
      death does.

But if only I could be certain that
      you were watching us
as we, at our best, watch one
      another,
with undemanding affection (now
      I find myself
asking more of you than any actor
      has a right to expect),
but if only I could be certain that
      when the worst happens,
as it will, I won't be alone,
      you'll be there,
you or someone like you, not to
      hold my hand,
not to touch me, not to whisper
      in my ear,
but merely to look on – how splendidly
      I might perform for you!

It's Good to Be Here

I'm in trouble, she said
to him. That was the first
time in history that anyone
had ever spoken of me.

It was 1932 when she
was just fourteen years old
and men like him
worked all day for
one stinking dollar.

There's quinine, she said.
That's bullshit, he told her.

Then she cried and then
for a long time neither of them
said anything at all and then
their voices kept rising until
they were screaming at each other
and then there was another long silence and then
they began to talk very quietly and at last he said,
well, I guess we'll just have to make the best of it.

While I lay curled up,
my heart beating,
in the darkness inside her.

At a Distance He Observes
an Unknown Girl Picking Flowers

If I think hard enough
of the roses and the girl
breaking them off,
of how the flowers would
smell if I touched them, taste if
I were a child again,
if I remember clearly
how the pain of a thorn differs
from other kinds (it's a little
like learning you've been
the victim of a small
disloyalty), if I convince myself
the girl is somebody
I've known well: Catherine
with whom I used to
bicycle to the Pratt
Farm, the pair of us
in bathing suits; I told her
about alewives, called
gaspereaux there, how we'd shipped them
south, salted, in barrels, more than
a century before, food
for slaves – convinced that
the knowledge made both
the fish and us
more important, a part
of what happened
in books; another time
we were stealing apples and I
mistook her ankle for a branch
of the tree, it was so dark, and
we fell to the ground together, young enough
that the pain of it only

excited us, that and the way
it was replaced slowly, by
the realisation that
the entire length of
our bodies touched,
which was like being thrown
into cold water and afterwards
drying off in the sun –
if I think hard enough it will appear
I've drawn something out
of the air, my mind pulling
invisible particles
together, forming a mass,
making.

The Social Worker's Poem

'You know them better,' said the girl,
whose face glowed with benevolence as from
too much cosmetics, speaking of the poor.
'What can you tell me that might help?'
She planned to do summer social work in a slum.

Do it as a bribe to God, I answered.
Do it because you hate
morons and dirty underwear. Do it because
you are one of those a sense of power causes
to breathe deeply and exhale aloud as if
it were a richer oxygen. Do it to cure
or satisfy some obscure sexual deviation.

But, above all, I said, don't act
from a desire to be loved. Don't ask
so great a payment for your services.
You'll wind up as bitter as the corner grocer
who gave too much credit and went bankrupt.

And remember, Miss, your admonishments
they'll find as irksome as
you're finding these of mine

Take my word for it. They're human.
Most of them will hate you.

The Rites of Manhood

It's snowing hard enough that the taxis aren't running.
I'm walking home, my night's work finished,
long after midnight, with the whole city to myself,
when across the street I see a very young American sailor
standing over a girl who's kneeling on the sidewalk
and refuses to get up although he's yelling at her
to tell him where she lives so he can take her there
before they both freeze. The pair of them are drunk
and my guess is he picked her up in a bar
and later they got separated from his buddies
and at first it was great fun to play at being
an old salt at liberty in a port full of women with
hinges on their heels, but by now he wants only to
find a solution to the infinitely complex
problem of what to do about her before he falls into
the hands of the police or the shore patrol
– and what keeps this from being squalid is
what's happening to him inside:
if there were other sailors here
it would be possible for him
to abandon her where she is and joke about it
later, but he's alone and the guilt can't be
divided into small forgettable pieces;
he's finding out what it means
to be a man and how different it is
from the way that only hours ago he imagined it.

The Jelly Bean Man

'He carries jelly beans,' a neighbour told us
when we first came here. 'You're lucky you don't
have any small children.'
                              He's the Jelly Bean Man
and the first words he ever said to me
were, 'Kiss it and make it well,'
he having observed my wife
bump her forehead against the door
of our car while getting into it
with her arms full of groceries.
'It's nothing to grin about,' he said.

So I kissed her above
and between the eyes, and he said,
'Love her; she is the daughter of
Cronos and Rhea, the sister and wife
of Zeus. Here I have a gift for her.
She will share it with you.'

And he insisted that she take
two cinnamon rolls
which she and I later ate
at home, very slowly,
with dairy butter
– each bite was like hearing
a little ripple of simple music.

Later we learned it was true
he carried jelly beans and distributed them,
but only as an uncle might or a grandfather
– and, oh, it's so easy to teach
your small daughters and sons
to accept nothing
from strangers, to keep well back always,

to stay out of arm's reach,
to be prepared to run,
so easy to tell them
about evil,
so hard to tell them
about innocence,

so impossible to say:
be good to the Jelly Bean Man
who gives candy to children
from no other motive than love.

He continues to try to avoid being caught

A memo to myself: Don't tell
anyone that a fiend from hell
bent over you last night and grinned.
Ask why you whimpered, blame the wind.

The Broadcaster's Poem

I used to broadcast at night
alone in a radio station
but I was never good at it,
partly because my voice wasn't right
but mostly because my peculiar
metaphysical stupidity
made it impossible
for me to keep believing
there was somebody listening
when it seemed I was talking
only to myself in a room no bigger
than an ordinary bathroom.
I could believe it for a while
and then I'd get somewhat
the same feeling as when you
start to suspect you're the victim
of a practical joke.
            So one part of me
was afraid another part
might blurt out something
about myself so terrible
that even I had never until
that moment suspected it.
            This was like the fear
of bridges and other
high places: Will I take off my glasses
and throw them
into the water, although I'm
half-blind without them?
Will I sneak up behind
myself and push?
            Another thing:
as a reporter
I covered an accident in which a train
ran into a car, killing

three young men, one of whom
was beheaded. The bodies looked
boneless, as such bodies do.
More like mounds of rags.
And inside the wreckage
where nobody could get at it
the car radio
was still playing.
                    I thought about places
the disc jockey's voice goes
and the things that happen there
and of how impossible it would be for him
to continue if he really knew.

Unfinished Poem

Bring me black slippers.
The corpse would dance.

The Middle-aged Man in the Supermarket

I'm pretending to test the avocadoes for ripeness
while gaping obliquely at the bare brown legs
of the girl in the orange skirt selecting mushrooms
when she says, 'Hi, there, let's make love.'
At first I think that she must have caught me
and is being sarcastic and then I decide
she's joking with someone she knows, perhaps the boy
        weighing green beans
or the young man with the watercress, so I try to act
as if I hadn't heard her, walk away at what I hope
is the right speed, without looking back,
and don't stop until I come to
the frozen-food bins, where I'm still standing,
gazing down at things I almost never buy, when
        I become aware
she's near me again, although I see only
a few square inches of brown thigh, a bit of orange cloth
and two symmetrical bare feet. I wish I could know
her body so well I could ever afterwards identify her
by taste alone. I rattle a carton
of frozen peas, read both French and English directions
on a package of frozen bread dough. She still stands there.
I wait for her to say to me:
'I fell in love the moment I saw you.
I want us to spend our first week together
in bed. We'll have our meals sent up. I'm even prettier
when I'm bare and I promise I'll keep my eyes shut
while you're naked, so that you'll never worry
that I might be comparing your body with that
of a previous lover, none of whom was older
than twenty, although the truth is I like
fat hips and big bellies – it's a kink that I have:
my nipples harden when I envision
those mountainous moons of flesh above me.'

In Praise of the Great Bull Walrus

I wouldn't like to be one
of the walrus people
for the rest of my life
but I wish I could spend
one sunny afternoon
lying on the rocks with them.
I suspect it would be similar
to drinking beer in a tavern
that caters to longshoremen
and won't admit women.
We'd exchange no
cosmic secrets. I'd merely say,
'How yuh doin' you big old walrus?'
and the nearest of
the walrus people
would answer,
'Me? I'm doin' great,
How yuh doin' yourself,
you big old human being, you?'
How good it is to share
the earth with such creatures
and how unthinkable it would have been
to have missed all this
by not being born:
a happy thought, that,
for not being born is
the only tragedy
that we can imagine
but need never fear.

My Beard, Once Lionheart Red

My beard, once Lionheart red, is now yellowish-gray
like a rainy sunset; a child, having seen the statue
in the Victoria and Albert Museum, of Silenus, the satyr
and foster father of Bacchus, and then noticing me
in the crowd, embarrassed her parents by pointing out
the resemblance; and yet, strange to say, I am happier
than when I was a boy and might have passed for the messenger
from Apollo to Helen, had I worn my hair long, and been naked,
        and had I known.

Happier, I suppose because I have all but abandoned hope of
        ever reaching
the lost island of answers, of ever catching up with the tribe
that left me behind as a baby, of meeting my real parents,
the King and Queen, of being adopted officially by God.

Happier, I suppose because I expect less and less
of everybody; where once I wanted all of creation to love me,
I am now almost content to have my presence acknowledged
with a semblance of kindness and a measure of grace.
I rarely make a nuisance of myself, as I so often used to do,
by passing out love, left and right, as if giving away kittens.

Happier, I suppose because I have tasted enough of fame
to know that it is not flavoured with sugar, as I had thought
when I studied it hungrily in pictures, but with salt;
and, also, that the potion does not transform the one who drinks it,
but instead creates for him an illusionary twin, in whose activities
his part, whether of proud or bemused brother,
is never more than peripheral; people seem to sense this,
for they treat him as if he were not altogether real,
will say to him, casually and with no apparent wish to be other
        than polite,
how amazing it is to find him so fat when he is known to be
        dying, slowly, of cancer.

Happier, I suppose because I was bound hand and foot,
          sewn in a blanket, thrown
into the pool of the man-eating crab, and broke free,
bearing wounds that will tug at me always, like the claws
of beggars, so that I cannot forget how wonderful it is
to get out of bed, stand up and walk, pick up a glass,
fill it with water, lift it to my mouth, and drink, with
          only enough pain
involved in each phase of the process to remind me that
          I am fortune's child, and richly blessed.

What Happened When He Went
to the Store for Bread

(for Michael Brian Oliver)

Because I went to the store for bread
one afternoon when I was eighteen
and arrived there just in time to meet
and be introduced to a man who had stopped
for a bottle of Coca-Cola (I've forgotten his name),
and because this man invited me to visit
a place where I met another man who gave me
the address of yet another man,
this one in another province,
and because I wrote a letter and got an answer
which took me away from the place where I was born,
I am who I am instead of being somebody else.

What would I have been if I hadn't left there
when I did? I would have almost certainly
gone mad; I think I might have killed somebody.
But even if something else had saved me
from madness, I would not be the same person.
I'd have spent thirty years in a different world
and come to look at things in such a different way
that even my memories of childhood and youth
would be different; it might even seem to me now
that there was never anything to escape from.

And then too, there are those who are other
than they would have been, because of some small act
of mine; I played a certain record once
because I liked it, and because he liked it too, a stranger
became my friend and, as such, met the woman
he married, and now they have two children
who would not have been born except for my taste in music.

Carrying the thought farther still, there must be
people in cities that I've never visited
whose lives have changed, perhaps not because of what
I've written but because I wrote: it might be
they didn't like my play and so left early
and because they left early something happened
that would not have happened if they'd stayed –
I put it that way so as not to sound immodest.
God knows, there's not a lot to boast about
when so much seems to depend upon the time of day
a boy goes out to buy a loaf of bread.

At the Head Table

Returning the same way as I went,
passing effortlessly and unnoticed
through the walls, I slip quietly back
inside my body, which is where I left it,
sitting on a chair in a large room, one among hundreds
of such bodies similarly seated
at long white tables that bear the remnants
of a meal, every face adjusted
so as to appear interested, but few wholly succeeding,
possibly because the owner is unskilful
or has drunk too much wine, or perhaps
because the equipment itself is faulty.

I check my watch; five minutes to go
before I start my speech. Here at the head table,
the Premier stirs and straightens;
he too has come back, it seems. The Bishop
is still far, far away, as are the Mayor,
the President of the University, and the two
members of Parliament. But they are all of them so adroit
at setting the controls on their bodies
for occasions such as this, that their neck and facial
muscles respond flawlessly; at intervals, each head
bobs as if in agreement, or cocks itself slightly
to one side, as if in polite dissent;
their lips open and close on cue, as if smiling,
while the toastmaster rattles on, quoting Churchill.

I ask myself, as every public speaker must,
should I stay here while being formally introduced,
or re-adjust my own face and risk another flight
out through the roof, across continents and centuries –

We found him kneeling

We found him kneeling under the front porch,
frozen to death. (Until now, he'd been hidden
by the deep snow.) He must have fallen asleep there
that night last winter when he left for Victoria.
(Once before he'd decided to bed down outdoors
on a winter's night: his mother had awakened me
at some godawful hour and said. 'You'll have to
do something, do you hear me, he'll die.'
That time she had happened to look out.) This time she cried
a little and then together we carried him
into the living-room and laid him down on the sofa.
He was wearing his uncle's tunic, designed
for the Maine State Troopers and worn
by the police in several little Canadian towns
along the border. There wasn't an ounce of flesh
on his bones and his skull was as thin as paper.
Then we remembered the telephone calls.
There was one only last night from Whitehorse.
Did that mean there was two of him,
one here and one there, and if so
would the other one die too when these
bones finally crumbled? I put his mother's
Hudson's Bay coat over him – and just in time:
his friends were outside, five or six of them
whom we hadn't seen in months, Ralph and the others,
standing in the fresh white snow.
as if keeping an appointment.

A Pair of Pruning Shears

The trees around this house are killing one
another. This summer, the maple and the fir
sucked the life from the spruce, having first
shut it off from the rain and then walled in its roots
with theirs, so that at last it died in a desert
five feet in diameter. The maple still
bears wounds from that struggle, a withered limb
for instance, and now the fir has turned against
its old ally and bars it from the sun,
while, a little distance away, the young birches
gnaw away at the beech and will bring her down
unless she succeeds in smothering them first;
and, afterwards, the winners will go at it –
'You ought to have pruned them,' a neighbour says,
who knows about such matters. 'It's the same
with everything,' he tells me. 'Even rhubarb.
Look at that fine patch you inherited from
the former tenants, gone to weed because
you didn't take a knife to it. It needed
to be cut back almost to the roots last season.
Now it's too late.' So I start with the rose-bushes
that were so elegant when we moved here but now
have sprouted hideous tentacles, each of them
black and bare except for a few red flowers
at the tip where, if this were a different kind
of horror story, there would be a mouth.
I take a knife, a saw, a pair of shears,
waiting until it's almost dark because,
being awkward at such tasks, I'd rather not
be watched, and drinking a quick double gin
because I'm loath to destroy anything,
never knowing where it might lead or end;
I take a knife, a saw, a pair of shears,
and soon I'm breathing hard and there is sweat

in my eyes and my heart is saying no, no, no,
reminding me that this body of mine is
a rickety Empire, in no shape for war,
Byzantium in 1450, Turkey
in 1914; I saw off the tentacles,
and scissor at the live, green undergrowth,
the thorns making me think of Gulliver
and the Lilliputian archers; there is blood
on my hands and forearms when I stop; the walk
is buried in debris, with a few spots
of red on the black and green: they're the flowers
that ought to have been mouths; because of them,
it is as if the bushes had bled too.

I'm still sitting there when the stars appear,
another drink beside me on the steps,
my rested heart now saying yes, no, yes,
but in a little while I'll go inside
to wait for spring. How good it would be then
to come out and look down at the black stumps
of the rose-bushes, stumps like rotten molars,
and see there in the grass a different shade
of green, one touched with gold, new growth,
the fresh stalks as supple as the partner in
a boy's lascivious dream, and glorious,
glorious and absurd, in the way of all
such living things that reach up to the sun
to touch it, though they've risen only scant
inches above the earth – an argument,
perhaps, although admittedly a weak one,
against the rumours, widespread and persuasive,
of Death's total, unconditional victory.

A Night in 1938, and the Night After

The first time I saw electric
light, the Queen of Heaven
appeared. This was not light
to see by, this was
light to marvel at. All
evening we sat, adults
as well as children, in that
light and did nothing
else. Next day we waited
for Uncle, as head of the
family, to decide the time
had come to switch it on
again. I held my breath
as he pulled the chain, but
the Queen of Heaven did not
return. In a little while,
the adults picked up
the playing cards. Oh!
how I despised them
for that. Then I saw
that the shadows were
gone, the places where
I could roll myself into
a ball or kneel or stand very
still, and not be seen.
I used to do that
and listen. Sometimes, I would
slip out of the shadows when
nobody was looking and
switch cards on them. It was hard
to keep from laughing then.
Now, no matter how
small, quick or quiet

I was, I would never
again have that power.
I could never again
make myself invisible.

Why are you crying?
Uncle asked me.

He Visits the Shrine of a Saint

Whenever I see the indentations left in granite
by the knees of generation after generation
of human beings, not all of them worshippers,
some of them, doubtless, only carrying out
what was then a social obligation, others not very
different from the poker player who gets up
when his luck is bad and, by way of incantation,
walks once around the table, still others whose purpose
was to please somebody, perhaps a parent out of kindness,
perhaps a superior out of fear or ambition
in an age when Mother Church could make an Emperor
or cause a King to submit to the lash,
whenever I look at such marks in a slab of stone
and reflect that most of those who helped to make them
have left no further trace of their passage,
it hardly matters to me whether faith or folly
moved them (when addressing mysteries for which
there are no words in any language, it seems only sensible
to give proper names to the more benign ones,
such as hope fulfilled, and to call them saints);
what does matter is that they came here, to this place,
and here performed a supremely human gesture;
I'm reminded of how Xerxes felt when he looked out at that
          vast army,
and it came to him that not one of them would be alive
in another hundred years; that was 2,500 years ago,
and he wept; but this is not so sad as that: when I envisage
all of those ardent pilgrims in the dust
and think of how they each made their minute imprint
and then vanished, thousands upon thousands
of them, none much wiser, none a bigger fool
than I have been, none guilty of a crime
I could not have committed, none much better
(not even the saint himself) than I might have been,

then I am almost at peace with the knowledge
of how quickly time will close the little space between us,
and my breath become one with theirs and the wind;
and so, laughing at myself as at any other
child doing something quaint, I say a prayer,
and might kneel down, if I could do it
without feeling fraudulent or being seen,
and if I could be certain that I had the right.

The Secretive Fishermen

It is dusk now, and the secretive fishermen
are trolling for boys on the highways
north and south of here: a tradition.
It is what you do when you work in a bank,
for instance, or for the government,
and share your neighbour's hunger but not his tastes.
You drive back and forth, back and forth,
in the twilight, and it can be dangerous;
men have been killed for it, and not one
of their murderers has ever been convicted.
Yet they are peaceable men, even timorous
about most things, men of moderate views
and modest ambitions, whose daytime dress
is always quietly correct; for the most part,
they have always lived here, and their fathers
worked for the bank or the government before them.
If they were married, it would be to women
much like their mothers, who belonged to
the usual organisations, cooked the usual meals,
and thought the usual thoughts. Instead,
out of necessity, the meek and mild accountant
rides out in search of adventure like
the Red Shadow, and Sir Percy Blakeney
risks death as the Scarlet Pimpernel,
except that this time the road is real,
just as the boys are not made of glossy paper
and therefore cannot be undressed
with a flick of the fingers turning over a page
nor be made to disappear in the same way:
they are co-authors and may change the script,
out of fear or disgust or because it amuses them,
so that it ends badly, with the Pimpernel
beaten bloody, the Red Shadow turned into
a monstrous parody of a baby-fat two-year-old,
blubbering, and naked except for an undershirt.

Still, it rarely comes to that; there must even be times
when it is almost perfect, in its way: two strangers,
each of them a tourist exploring the Mexico
that is the other's body. It can't always be
as sad as dusk for those lonesome travellers.

I'm Simply Walking

I'm simply walking,
I think.
Or standing there.
I'm not afraid,
which means the
homicidal maniac
must be dead.

I can't tell where I am,
but that is only because
there has been no reason
for me to ask myself:
what place is this?

Nothing horrible
has happened.

I'm simply walking,
except
this time I'm not a man;
I'm a woman.

The most extraordinary
thing about this
is that it is
of no importance.

Perhaps that's because
there's nobody else here.

I put one foot in front
of the other
and think no more
about being a woman
than a woman would.

If I'm wearing a dress,
well, what of it,
I must be accustomed to
wearing dresses.

It's nothing at all like
putting on your sister's
panties and frock
when you were twelve
and wanting to be seen
like that,
but please God never
recognised.

Watch me, Sir
Looking Glass!
You said then,
and twirled
like a top

until you thought
how awful it must be
to bleed like that.

Legacy

(adapted from the Romanian of Tudor Arghezi)

All that I'll leave you when I die is a name in a book
which they'll say is mine. Take it in the long evening
which stretches all the way from my farthest ancestors to you,
across the ravines and ditches which they bridged or climbed,
and you too, so young, are expected to conquer.
The book is only a single step, yet it is your solemn charter,
won by slaves and serfs who strained beneath their loads:
sacks filled with their own bones, handed down to me.

So that I could change a spade into a pen,
our ancestors suffered together with their oxen,
and gathered the sweat of a hundred years to give me ink.
I kneaded the words that they spoke to their cattle
until they were transformed into visions and icons.
Out of their rags, I made wreaths; and from old poisons
I made honey. From their hearths I took
the ashes of the dead and made them live again
in a god of stone and paper who holds the world
in his lap and watches over you.

All the pain and sorrow of our people
I put into a single violin
and as the master heard it played
he danced like a he-goat in the spring.
We withstood the whip, and now the lash turns into words
and becomes a live growth that spreads in the air,
bearing at its tip, like a grape, the fruit
of ancient and endless sorrow.

However soft her bed may be when she reads it,
the Princess will suffer in my book;
for words of fire and steel are mingled with the soft whisper
in the book that a slave wrote and the lord reads without knowing
that in its depths there lies all the rage of my forefathers.

He Reflects Upon His Own Stupidity

(for Michael Pacey)

For the first twenty-five years of my life
I never met anyone who was stupid
in quite the same way as I am.

Oh, I knew many, many people
who would have been judged subnormal
by a professional psychologist
– for whatever that is worth:
not much, I imagine, since almost all
the professional psychologists I've run into
have been lunatics or fools.

But I never met anyone who was an idiot
about doors, as I am. I turn my hotel key
this way and that, that way and this,
can seldom get out of a car without help.

If we were measured by our success with locks,
I would be assessed as possibly trainable,
but certainly not educable.

I'm equally stupid about many other things.
And, dear God, it used to be lonely.

But now almost everyone I know is stupid
in much the same way as I am.
Not merely my friends but casual acquaintances,
yes, and enemies too, keep locking themselves out,
and getting lost,
and have trouble changing a tyre.

My stupidity matches theirs.
I have found my tribe and am more at home in the world.

Subway Psalm

It's the first storm of the winter
and the worst since 1888,
the girl on television said.

I keep slipping in my leather-soled shoes.
Twice I've turned into a windmill
in my efforts to keep from falling.

At the top of the stairs leading down
to the subway, Johnnie watches me,
not just with his eyes but with his arms and legs.
He'll do his best to save the old man.

That's how I must have looked at him
when he was five or six years old.
Now he's twenty-six, and it seems
we've traded places.
                    Why are you laughing?
he asks me.
            The honest answer is:
Because you look so funny, standing there
like that, my beautiful son,
and because I've loved you
for such a long time and because this
is the finest storm I've ever seen
and everything is exactly as it should be.

Great Things Have Happened

We were talking about the great things
that have happened in our lifetimes;
and I said, 'Oh, I suppose the moon landing
was the greatest thing that has happened
in my time.' But, of course, we were all lying.
The truth is the moon landing didn't mean
one-tenth as much to me as one night in 1963
when we lived in a three-room flat in what once had been
the mansion of some Victorian merchant prince
(our kitchen had been a clothes closet, I'm sure),
on a street where by now nobody lived
who could afford to live anywhere else.
That night, the three of us, Claudine, Johnnie and me,
woke up at half-past four in the morning
and ate cinnamon toast together.

'Is that all?' I hear somebody ask.

Oh, but we were silly with sleepiness
and, under our windows, the street-cleaners
were working their machines and conversing in Italian, and
everything was strange without being threatening,
even the tea-kettle whistled differently
than in the daytime: it was like the feeling
you get sometimes in a country you've never visited
before, when the bread doesn't taste quite the same,
the butter is a small adventure, and they put
paprika on the table instead of pepper,
except that there was nobody in this country
except the three of us, half-tipsy with the wonder
of being alive, and wholly enveloped in love.

How Beautiful Art Thy Feet with Shoes

I suppose it's because so many
poets and artists have never had enough
love from women – as boys they were hideous
in their own eyes, as I was, who thought myself
half-brother to Quasimodo
and looked upon every girl as Esmeralda –
I suppose it's because of this
that they've devoted so much time
to portraying the wonders
of her nakedness, to celebrating
her thighs and breasts
so that some love poems sound more like
commercials for fried chicken,
and hardly ever mention
moments like this when I look up and see you,
through the window, getting out of a cab
with your arms full of Christmas parcels
(they always seem to be
Christmas parcels, even in July and even if
they're only books from the public library)
there must have been times, many times,
over the years, when you came home from somewhere
without your arms filled with parcels,
but I don't remember any of them now,
nor do I recall a time when you didn't come in
either bursting to show me something
or trying to hide something from me:
I've never known anybody so fond of arranging
surprises or so inept at keeping secrets;
and I know how long it takes you to complete
the smallest transaction, how much you like to
look at things and touch them, and how you're always
getting involved in long conversations with
old men in waiting-rooms, little kids on tricycles,

the high school students who work part-time in supermarkets,
how you even say, 'Hello, dog', if you meet one –
all this, and so much more, goes through my head
as I catch a glimpse of you, getting out of a cab
with your arms full of parcels, as they always are,
and am reminded, suddenly, of how much I love you.

A poem for Aida Flemming

May God have mercy
on the porcupine
broken free
but with the snare
still around his neck,
the end of it trailing
behind him
and bound to catch
on something,

on the skunk also
with her head
hopelessly stuck
in a tomato tin,

and the bird who won't
let me pick her up
before the cat comes,

and all other creatures
trapped
and too frightened
to allow anyone to help.

Bobby Sands
(for Robert Weaver)

I did not cry for Bobby Sands, but I almost did,
thinking of my grandmother whom I loved, and who loved me,
and of how her voice would break when she told me again
how her grandmother died in a field in County Wexford
with green stains on her lips, her hands filled with grass,
and of how in that same year the English wagons
escorted by English troops carried Irish grain
down to English vessels for shipment to England. Yes,
yes, that was a long, long time ago; but somebody should
remember Mary Foley, somebody should weep for her,
even if it is only a drunken listener
to lying ballads. Being human, we
each of us can bear no more than a particle
of pain that is not our own; the rest is rhetoric.
Better to shed a tear for Mary Foley
than to rant or babble about suffering
that is beyond our capacity to comprehend.
And what of Bobby Sands? We talk too much,
all of us. In common decency, don't speak
of him unless you have gone at least a day
without food, and be sure you understand
that he loved being alive, the same as you.
Then say what you like. Call him a fool.
Call him a criminal. You'll get no argument
from me. I'll agree with everything
you say in dispraise of gunmen. Oh, but Mary Foley's
ghost was left in my keeping.
I know in my heart that if he had come to me
for a place to hide I could never have shut him out.

He Sits Down on the Floor of a School
for the Retarded

I sit down on the floor of a school for the retarded,
a writer of magazine articles accompanying a band
that was met at the door by a child in a man's body
who asked them, 'Are you the surprise they promised us?'

It's Ryan's Fancy, Dermot on guitar,
Fergus on banjo, Denis on penny-whistle.
In the eyes of this audience, they're everybody
who has ever appeared on TV. I've been telling lies
to a boy who cried because his favourite detective
hadn't come with us; I said he had sent his love
and, no, I didn't think he'd mind if I signed his name
to a scrap of paper: when the boy took it, he said,
'Nobody will ever get this away from me,'
in the voice, more hopeless than defiant,
of one accustomed to finding that his hiding places
have been discovered, used to having objects snatched
out of his hands. Weeks from now I'll send him
another autograph, this one genuine
in the sense of having been signed by somebody
on the same payroll as the star.
Then I'll feel less ashamed. Now everyone is singing,
'Old MacDonald had a farm,' and I don't know what to do

about the young woman (I call her a woman
because she's twenty-five at least, but think of her
as a little girl, she plays that part so well,
having known no other), about the young woman who
sits down beside me and, as if it were the most natural
thing in the world, rests her head on my shoulder.

It's nine o'clock in the morning, not an hour for music.
And, at the best of times, I'm uncomfortable
in situations where I'm ignorant
of the accepted etiquette: it's one thing

138

to jump a fence, quite another thing to blunder
into one in the dark. I look around me
for a teacher to whom to smile out my distress.
They're all busy elsewhere. 'Hold me,' she whispers. 'Hold me.'

I put my arm around her. 'Hold me tighter.'
I do, and she snuggles closer. I half-expect
someone in authority to grab her
or me; I can imagine this being remembered
for ever as the time the sex-crazed writer
publicly fondled the poor retarded girl.
'Hold me,' she says again. What does it matter
what anybody thinks? I put my other arm around her,
rest my chin in her hair, thinking of children
real children, and of how they say it, 'Hold me,'
and of a patient in a geriatric ward
I once heard crying out to his mother, dead
for half a century, 'I'm frightened! Hold me!'
and of a boy-soldier screaming it on the beach
at Dieppe, of Nelson in Hardy's arms,
of Frieda gripping Lawrence's ankle
until he sailed off in his Ship of Death.

It's what we all want, in the end,
to be held, merely to be held,
to be kissed (not necessarily with the lips,
for every touching is a kind of kiss).

Yes, it's what we all want, in the end,
not to be worshipped, not to be admired,
not to be famous, not to be feared,
not even to be loved, but simply to be held.

She hugs me now, this retarded woman, and I hug her.
We are brother and sister, father and daughter,
mother and son, husband and wife.
We are lovers. We are two human beings
huddled together for a little while by the fire
in the Ice Age, two hundred thousand years ago.

A Song To Be Whispered

Your body consists of so many provinces
that I, a man of salt, must break off my fingers
one by one –
                    like so!

See how they fly,
become birds in an orchard.

Oh, my love, it was
God Himself who wove
the skin that clothes you.

Yet the eunuch who escorts
Bathsheba to the King's House
mutters, as always,
'No good can come of it.'

You Can't Get There from Here

There is almost always a lilac bush – lilac was the smell
of my childhood, a fine free smell that sets colts galloping
along cool rivers in my mind – and there are almost always
red rose bushes and, sometimes, an apple tree
or even an orchard, where the deer feed on windfalls; and in
       the tall grass
you may come upon a pair of sheep shears, like monstrous
       scissors but made in one piece
as tweezers are, and a grub-hoe, like a two-bitted axe
except that one bit is a hammer; and if you dare to go inside
what remains of the house, there could be a schooner
on the floor at the head of the stairs to the cellar,
its three-foot-long hull on its side, its masts broken, its rigging
rotted; and we'll be there watching
from the dark by the vegetable bins – there was never any
light to switch on, and you'll not have brought with you
a lantern to find us,
but we will see you; oh, we will see you.

1914-1918

Thinking again of all those young men who were given the same
      first name,
Canada, once they had reached the place which we in our
      innocence then
called *Overseas*, doubtless with the same intonation
as Frankish peasants had used eight centuries earlier
in speaking of the sons who had followed their steely Lords to
      Outre Mar;
thinking of how a German officer remembered this for half a
      century as the strangest thing
he saw in four years of war – the Canadians walking,
simply walking, in no apparent order, but like any group of men
      going anywhere,
into a hailstorm of machine-gun fire that flattened them like wheat,
'They did not even look like soldiers, yet fought like Prussian
      Guards,'
I wish, as they would have done, who were much like me,
though they were so much younger, that God's bad brother,
having killed them, had said *Enough!* and had not proceeded
to prove their deaths were pointless; if they had to die
(and all of us do; oh, all of us do), then I wish
that we could say that we are who we are because they were who
      they were,
That much, at least, has been given others. I think of names:
Salamanca, Antietam, Leningrad. I think of Polish miners
singing of Polish horsemen, a Cuban schoolchild placing flowers
at a wall filled with old photographs.
                        All of it lies,
perhaps, or romantic rubbish, though those young men would not
      have thought it was.

My country has no history, only a past.

The Writer-in-Residence's Poem

He was one of those kids who say they want to be poets.
'This one is pompous and not overly bright,' I thought
as I thumbed through the typewritten lists he had handed me
of words like 'lonely' and 'love' and 'Apocalypse',
and listened to him say he knew he had talent and only wanted
            to be told
whether he was heading in the right direction.

The worst of it was he didn't know when to go – and knowing
            when to go is far more important
than being talented or wearing clean underwear.
He sat in my living-room for one hour, two hours, three –
with me aching to say, 'Go away, please, you're making me so
            lonely
that if you don't leave soon I may burst into tears.'

Still he stayed.
                He had an irritating manner
of putting his hand in front of his mouth and half-turning away
            when he spoke
as if afraid of what might come out,
and when I spoke to him, which was less and less often
as the evening wore on, he scowled as if concentrating
so hard it was painful.

'Thank God, that's over,' I thought when he left.
It wouldn't have been so bad if it hadn't been
for those disgusting mannerisms. Then I realised why
his gestures had seemed so familiar – that hand
in front of the mouth, those shifty eyes, that scowl;
and I almost ran after and embraced the poor bugger.
For he had been labouring to be me –
me in the flesh, I mean, out of his longing
for what he innocently imagined me to possess
and believed that he wanted to be.

Driving a Hard Bargain

What would cause a man to haggle over the price
of the rifle which, later that same day,
he used to kill himself?
                              As a young reporter,
I thought, 'Capitalism!'
                              The poor bastard knew what it was
to ask the landlord if he'd wait another week, and then
thank him for answering, 'I don't seem to have much choice
in the matter, do I?' in the tone of voice
and with the facial expression of a gentleman
on horseback tapping his boot with a whip,
knew what it was like to make his wife cry every payday
as men on low wages almost always do (it begins with an
          argument
over some small luxury – perhaps a gift one has bought for
          the other, a bottle of wine
to celebrate her birthday, a colour TV she has secretly rented
for him to watch the Grey Cup game – and the realisation
that because of it something else will now have to be
endured or postponed or done without or given up.)
'No,' the sales clerk said. 'This guy was loaded.'
'Drunk?' 'Nah, loaded with dough. And guess how much
he made me knock off the price. Are you ready for this?
Two measly bucks.'
                              Could it have been habit then?
I once knew the owner of a substantial business
who, after his secretary had gone home, searched through the
          wastebaskets
for envelopes that bore uncancelled postage stamps.
The same man had gone in at night or on a weekend
and, with a screwdriver, adjusted the softdrink machines,
so that they'd not disgorge the bottle-caps,
some of which were worth two dollars in a contest.
He might have dickered in the face of death.

I don't know. I do know that for twenty years
I've wondered about that man who killed himself.
Perhaps, when in the store, he was not yet aware
of how he would use the rifle. Perhaps he expected
to go on a hunting trip with friends. Enough can happen
in an hour to make a man decide he'd rather
be dead.

Or, for whatever reason, would he still be
alive if the clerk had refused to sell for any less?

Home from the Wars

(for Walter Learning)

His hand in his mother's, her
scented with dried rose petals
and spearmint, the whole city
turned upside down, spilling out a torrent
of people, the flood rushing down
to the harbour where even the cloth flags
joined in the clapping and the ships' horns
wallowed in it –

'There's your father!' she said.
But there were so many,
all the same greenish-brown
scum and mud colour,
so many of them on the decks
of the troopship, looking down
as if from a cloud in a nightmare,
every last one of them
judging him,
it seemed, and his mother
had let go.

          But he didn't cry
until he hung suspended
in the air while the stranger's
coarse wool sandpapered his face;
and he's not sure if it was then
or in memory years afterwards that he saw
a gull die in each of the man's eyes
as they do when small boys with fishing lines
hook them
          and he cried again.

He Attempts to Love His Neighbours

My neighbours do not wish to be loved.
They have made it clear that they prefer to go peacefully
about their business and want me to do the same.
This ought not to surprise me as it does;
I ought to know by now that most people have a hundred things
they would rather do than have me love them.

There is television, for instance; the truth is that almost
      everybody,
given the choice between being loved and watching TV,
would choose the latter. Love interrupts dinner,
interferes with mowing the lawn, washing the car,
or walking the dog. Love is a telephone ringing or a doorbell
waking you moments after you've finally succeeded in getting
      to sleep.

So we must be careful, those of us who were born with
the wrong number of fingers or the gift
of loving; we must do our best to behave
like normal members of society and not make nuisances
of ourselves; otherwise it could go hard with us.
It is better to bite back your tears,
swallow your laughter,
and learn to fake the mildly self-deprecating titter
favoured by the bourgeoisie
than to be left entirely alone, as you will be,
if your disconformity embarrasses
your neighbours; I wish I didn't keep forgetting that.

He Enters His 50th Year

Nine-tenths blind without my glasses
and growing deafer every year
(they tell me it's hereditary),

threatened with diabetes, forced out of bed
by my bladder two or three times a night
(they tell me this is the surcharge
on all those forty-ouncers of gin),

bursitis in my elbow, receding gums, a loose tooth
(my doctor and dentist advise me to put up with it
as long as I can and then they'll try something
which, they warn, will quite possibly make it worse),

I feel myself dissolving like a snowman,
coming to pieces like an old book.
But I'm not complaining.
It is not as bad as it sounds.
There are compensations.

For one thing, I've accumulated such a company
of past selves, enough of them to fill the stage
in a sizeable theatre, that it is easier to believe
the person I am is only one among many, to look at him
in almost the same way I would look at anyone else.

For another thing, I can now laugh out loud
at incidents such as my first time with a girl
I knew would let me do it. Having read Havelock Ellis,
I knew about foreplay. Oh! My hands and mouth did
ingenious things to her 15-year-old body.
I remember especially a game with her thighs, the prescription
called for the fingers to tiptoe ever so slowly
towards the root of her womanhood, touch it so deftly

and retreat so swiftly she could not be sure
whether what she felt was real or imagined,
then to begin again, insect-like, at her knees.

That worked perfectly. She lay moist and squirming,
eyes screwed shut, mouth open – and then
I couldn't get it up. I couldn't get it up.
Havelock Ellis hadn't warned me
this might happen. I wanted to die.
How I wanted to die. And afterwards, alone in bed
I thought for a long time about various ways
of killing myself. Good God, what if she told
somebody?
      I address the rest of this:
to the boy I was: I could never laugh at you unkindly.

The Sculpin

'Like an orgasm,' I thought, watching the weir fishermen
empty their nets of herring, an onrush of life
spouting into the hold of a boat, and the boat rocking.
And, later, 'if only human beings died as it seems to us that
            herring do,
swept away by their dance, their bodies mirrors for the sun.'
But that was later; though the fish were dying, thousands of them,
swimming frantically in the air that to them is nothingness,
while I watched the weirmen at work I no more thought of death
than of the children who might have been born of the sperm
            I wasted.

Yet, I had cursed myself and the two American women
fishing with rods from the wharf's edge. They were harmless
            creatures,
tourists like me, and had hooked a sculpin,
a fish to which they bore a macabre resemblance,
being bloated and with strange protrusions and colorations.
Their jokes about its ugliness ought to have been funny,
and might have been, except that it lay writhing
at their feet, while they laughed their horrible
Pink Lady and Bingo Night laughs, and kept poking it:
God, how I hated their fingernail-polished toenails, and myself
            for not
rescuing their victim; I had wanted to
elbow them aside, somehow remove the hook,
put the fish back, gently, in its own element.

'The difference is in attitudes,' a part of me says.
The weirmen are so sparing of everything, even words and
            movements;
nothing is wasted. They would understand
those old breech-clouted hunters said to have asked
forgiveness of their kill. I suppose the truth
is that when I saw the herring, I saw herring,
and when I saw the sculpin, I saw myself.

My Father's Body Was Found by Children

My father's body was
found by children.
Boys from the neighbourhood
who thought he was asleep
in his chair until
they came back next day
and saw he hadn't moved.
Children often visited him,
I'm told. He'd wrestle
with them if he was drunk,
converse with them soberly
at other times. His shack
was the sort of dwelling
a twelve-year-old would
build for himself,
in his last years he lived
the way a small boy would
if allowed to live alone.
Huck Finn at seventy.

To think he might have been
a child all his life
if less had been asked
of him and more been given.

To think I'm afraid
of him, even now,
half-expecting to look out
some night and see him
standing there:
I fear that most.

The All Night Diner

The man in the next booth pleads for forgiveness.
Each time our eyes meet I read the same questions:
Who am I? How did I get here? What have I done?
What must I do to make you love me again?

And we're almost strangers. Though I've seen enough
to know he's the kind of drunk who can hold down a job
by working twice as hard as anybody else
days he's sober enough to work:
                                        his face is the same
as those of the winos who spend every day
making chin music on the riverbank
back of the Chinese laundry, but their hands are as soft
as a priest's or a banker's. Not his. After forty years
of punching stone walls to prove he's a man,
of clutching that last shred of dignity
that won't let him spill a drop of his hot pork gravy
(first food in three days) though every blood vessel
burst with the effort of keeping the spoon from shaking.
There can come a time
when holding a spoon like a man will save a man's soul.

Confession

Beloved, it frightens me
how all things circle and meet.

I have singled you out
from all the world.

When you lie naked beneath me
or when only our fingertips
touch on the street,
I love you so gently
I become a saint
and would preach to the birds,
had they no better music.

Yet nothing is simple:
all things circle and meet.

The man who took his pleasure
of the young girl's body
and then strangled her
and threw her in a sewer
like a used condom –

there was a moment
before he gave way
to terror
when he studied her knees
like a famished boy,
an instant when he noted
how the spring wind
played with her hair
like young deer in a wheatfield
(he too was a sentimentalist)

and I, beloved,
lightly kissing your breasts
(do you remember, my little jester,
how you told me once
to be less gentle
with the sacred grotto
between your thighs
because, darling, it won't break)

might love you less
if I did not know
that other so well
had not talked with him
far into the night.

This Is What I Wanted to Sign Off With

You know what I'm
like when I'm sick: I'd sooner
curse than cry. And people don't often
know what they're saying in the end.
Or I could die in my sleep.

So I'll say it now. Here it is.
Don't pay any attention
if I don't get it right
when it's for real. Blame that
on terror and pain
or the stuff they're shooting
into my veins. This is what I wanted to
sign off with. Bend
closer, listen, I love you.

GREGORY M. COOK

The Wine of Astonishment

ALDEN NOWLAN, 1933-1983

Many, many times since I was a very small child I've stopped for moment and thought to myself how very strange it is to be alive, that recurrent feeling of naked wonder.

– ALDEN NOWLAN, 1981

Alden Nowlan is born in the backwoods of Hants County, Nova Scotia, on 25 January 1933, in the middle of Canada's Depression. His father, 29, works for $1 a day. Alden's mother turns 15, the March after his birth. This is her ninth home. The modest Nowlan house sits on a small patch of farmland at the forest's edge.

The marriage ends during the war. By then Alden has learned to read and write – before he starts school, while living at his maternal grandmother's. When his grandmother dies, his mother leaves the village. Back at his father's and his paternal grand-mother's home, the boy in short pants sees a movie-life of writer Jack London. Dreaming fame, Alden begins writing poems. Accused of plagiarism, he drops out of school aged 12.

To others it's as though he has left the village, except for the lamplight in the window where he scribbles. His first published letter to a paper appears in 1946. But grandmother Nowlan is dying. When the doctor makes his last call in 1947, he finds Alden anaemic and depressed – severely enough to be hospitalised.

Back home in 1948 Alden turns to labour: peeling pulp, doing farm chores. Four more letters are published. He writes diaries, essays, and fiction. CBC radio is his high school.

In 1949 a public library opens, 30 miles away, in Windsor. The librarian recognises an 'outstanding mind'. Extended privileges not offered adults, Alden feeds on literary masters.

For 25 cents an hour he is given a job as night watch on the sawmill boiler. He buys a $50 typewriter by mail order. Leaving the mill, he cuts brush for the department of highways.

In 1951 an American magazine accepts one of his poems. Six of his letters appear in journals. The *Windsor Tribune*, recognising Alden's talent and commitment, engages him as a book reviewer and correspondent. Claiming a high school diploma, adding a year to his age, and writing his own letter of reference, Alden is hired by mail as a newspaper reporter in Hartland, New Brunswick: 'It was as if I'd opened / Grimms' Fairy Tales and lowered myself into / one of the illustrations, become / the stripling taking his leave / of his village' ('He Takes His Leave': *see* 90-91).

The weekly *Observer* starts him at $27.50 a week. Hartland is a finishing school: 'I began to enjoy a more social life. For the first time I was not looked upon as a freak.' Travelling for fish and game conservation meetings, writing for farm magazines, managing a touring band, he experiences New Brunswick at its roots.

His 23rd year is magical. He falls in love with Claudine Orser, a new typesetter at the *Observer*.

Poetry prizes – books, or $5 here or there – arrive. His poems are broadcast in California where his first poetry chapbook is solicited. His first sale of a short story fetches $3 from *Queen's University Quarterly*.

For Alden, poetry's power is simplicity: 'the greatest wonder of poetry is that it combines toughness with the tenderness of love, and the one is impossible without the other.'

His first poetry reading in Toronto is scheduled. Two more books of poetry are announced. He begins his first novel. A Canada Council fellowship of $2000 is awarded him in June of 1961.

As political activist, Alden chairs a committee to save a man from the gallows. He quits the *Observer* until the grant money runs out. But no publisher takes his novel, *The Wanton Troopers* (1985). New Brunswick Premier Richard Hatfield recalls that Alden is so hurt that he threatens to find a way to return the Canada Council money. Feeling holed-up in Hartland, the child of the Depression is almost too insecure to leave. He finds strength, however, in the power of his maturing poetry and his compassion for Claudine and John, her nine-year-old son.

He is close to despair when we first meet in 1963, and he gives me an interview, explaining his crisis. Economically, he is no better off than when he peeled pulp. He accepts a job on the *Telegraph-Journal* in Saint John at $75 a week.

There is a marriage to arrange, debts to settle, and the room – in which he has lived for ten years with about 1,000 books – to sort out. The city is a relative cosmopolitan delight, yet Alden is spiritually enriched even when it seems: '…that there was nobody in this country / except the three of us, half-tipsy with the wonder / of being alive, and wholly enveloped in love.' ('Great Things Have Happened': 133).

Made provincial editor, Alden moves to night desk, telling me he is: 'Working my guts out. I wish to God I wasn't so damn loyal.' Promoted to news editor, Alden arrives at a 'living wage' for the first time in his life.

Six months later, March 1966, he is diagnosed with thyroid cancer. Following three operations, he is released in May. The thyroid gland gone, the severed jugular vein repaired; many nerves and muscles damaged, he gives primary credit for his life to his wife and son. There are radiation treatments. It's painful to type.

But the poems keep coming, like new friends we seem to have known all our lives: 'what if / I die / and go home / and Claudine is crying: / will she know / what it means / even if I / have the strength / to knock / a pencil off the table?' ('Morning of the Third Operation': 53-54).

He receives grants from both Guggenheim Foundation and Canada Council, and signs book contracts for new poems and his first collection of stories. His facial features altered by surgery, Alden grows a beard. As part of his convalesence, he makes the first of two visits to England and ancestral Ireland.

Bread, Wine and Salt is published. It's Canada's centennial. Invitations to conferences and readings increase. Radio and book anthologists solicit his work. Each exposure adds to Alden's sense of vulnerability. But, as he explains to novelist Raymond Fraser, much of poetry's obscurity is a defensive mechanism to avoid this confessional voice – the voice that Alden feels is essential.

1968 brings news that he has won Canada's most prestigious poetry award – the Governor General's. The Canada Council supports the University of New Brunswick's request for Alden as writer-in-residence.

Having contemplated his own death nearly every day for the past two years, as if outwitting an assassin stalking him, Alden finds the satire of his earlier writing turning into gentler – even hilarious – comfort for anyone who can laugh at himself.

Robert Bly, who calls Alden Nowlan 'the greatest Canadian poet of the 20th century', introduces him to U.S. readers as one of those writers who alter how a civilisation sees itself. Canada's premier regional and national magazines, radio and television enlist him as writer and subject. He writes speeches for the new Premier, his old friend Richard Hatfield.

UNB bestows an Honorary D. Litt, and the Premier's office supplants the Canada Council funding for Alden's chair. The first Masters thesis on him is completed. Son, John, leaves home for college.

1973-74 is a watershed: his fourth book of poems and a novel are published, as well as short works and speeches. In the middle of it Alden's father dies at 70 years, 11 July 1974, six days before his *Frankenstein* has its stage première. And Alden meets his heroes, Johnny Cash and June Carter, with Prince Charles.

An Honorary Doctor of Laws comes from Dalhousie University (1976).

'Utterly exhausted', he returns from yet another reading tour. He and Claudine visit Cuba. Distinctions continue, with medals for drama, prose and poetry. The University of Calgary opens negotiations to acquire his papers, and the West Hants Historical Society (1980) raises a plaque in the Windsor library.

He asks poet Irving Layton if he has chosen a title for his autobiography, offering his own: *The Wine of Astonishment* from 'thou hast made us drink the wine of astonishment (Psalms 60:3).'

Alden's medical condition is balanced between two doctors in different cities. He tells a third physician-friend: 'When I'm dying I don't want any of your quackery or advice. I want you to play checkers with me.'

Dieting and trying to keep a chemical balance for various threats to his health, he writes, in 'My Beard Once Lionheart Red' (114-15) of 'how wonderful it is / to get out of bed, stand up and walk, pick up a glass, / fill it with water, lift it to my mouth, and drink, with only enough pain / involved in each phase of the process to remind me that I am fortune's child, and richly blessed'.

On 11 June, he awakes and struggles for breathe. He insists on dressing for, and walking to, the ambulance. A full pulmonary-cardiac arrest – and complications in resuscitation owing to old scar tissues – leave him in a coma. On 27 June 1983, he dies from pneumonia, aged 50.